YELLOW SPAGHETTI

Michael Needham

First published 2018
by Rowanvale Books Ltd
The Gate
Keppoch Street
Roath
Cardiff
CF24 3JW
www.rowanvalebooks.com

A CIP catalogue record for this book is available from the British Library.
ISBN: 978-1-912655-08-3

To my niece, Skye. I hope this book will help you on your journey. Dyspraxia has not stopped me achieving things, and I'm sure you will achieve everything you can.

INTRODUCTION

I love my family dearly and am forever grateful for the quality of my upbringing, which very much taught me right from wrong, and the amazing family holidays that influenced my love of all things travel.

You don't need to read the chapters of this book in the printed order; you can start with the ones that interest you more. The chapters are quite diverse. There is also pictorial content on Facebook—you don't need to have a Facebook account to access it, it's just an easy way of including photos.

My inspiration for writing this book was a documentary on Amazon. I loved the simplicity that you no longer have to face rejection by loads of publishing houses—you can simply write a book and get it published. There is a book in everyone!

I can't promise this will be an error-free book. While hours of editing have taken place, my dyslexia/dyspraxia is likely to mean I will miss some mistakes. Feel free to circle/use red pen for any errors! If mistakes annoy you, perhaps this isn't the book for you!

CONTENTS

CHAPTER 1

My Mum's Account of my Early Years
Moira Needham

Monday, 23 September 1974
The first signs of labour came at seven-thirty in the morning. At 1 p.m. Douglas took me to Newcastle General Hospital and, four hours later, baby Michael arrived! (I'd known since I was a teenager that I would name my first son Michael.) We were separated quite quickly, and I wasn't able to hold my baby for another seventeen hours. When he was brought to me in his Perspex crib, he unfurled his right hand and the bottom fell out of my world. Michael had his two middle fingers joined from tip to base—my baby wasn't perfect. (But there was no doubt he was my baby, as he was a squished-up version of my dad.)

The next morning, Douglas brought us home. Michael was quite jaundiced (as his sister had been). He was not very interested in feeding, but the weather was nice, and the health visitor suggested—for both our benefits—that I take him out a walk in his pram.

For the next week, I more or less stayed in my bedroom with Michael—I think the health visitor may have been to visit again during this period? On day ten, the doctor visited, took one look at my floppy baby and called an ambulance.

The next week was hell. They stopped me breastfeeding, but Michael didn't take much from the bottle. He was often sick, and in the early hours of one morning, he was sick on the floor. On studying the bottle, I realised the milk was out of date. I was now hysterical and being told off by the nurse!

Later that day, a decision was made to start antibiotics. He did have a lumbar puncture at some point, but the decision to give him antibiotics was made, with them implying it may or may not be the right decision but was worth a try. Michael slowly recovered and came back home at twenty days old, and life with my baby started again.

Unfortunately, I was becoming very unwell mentally. Fortunately, Michael's sister, Carole, was there for him. Carole is almost eighteen months older than him. She had been unsettled, naturally, when I was in hospital with Michael, but once we were back home, she became a second "mum" to him. She has looked out for Michael all his life; they have a special relationship.

After this start to his life, Michael continued to be floppy, not sitting unaided till he was about eighteen months old. He took his first steps at over twenty-one months, which was so thrilling! We were on holiday with friends in Kirkcudbright, and we immediately shopped for smart blue shoes. To this day, Michael walking was a huge moment in our lives.

Michael, almost three, started nursery. He was very cute, with white-blonde hair. He was very popular, but Jennifer was his special pal.

The November after starting playgroup, the decision was made to separate Michael's conjoined fingers. The operation was carried out in Dundee

Royal Infirmary. The surgery was very successful, although he would never write with his right hand, even though he was meant to be right-handed. He never cried in hospital—it was like he didn't feel pain. It was an anxious time keeping his wound clean and his thigh (where the donor skin came from) dry. It would be a while before he was out of his night-time nappies.

From 1975 till 1981 we lived in Broughty Ferry. Our doctor was not very supportive—did he think I was a neurotic mother because of my depression?!

In the daytime, he was generally happy, but night-times would be a problem until he was four. He cried every night, which was difficult. He seemed to just want me with him. He didn't like soft toys in his bedroom—he thought his toy Womble was alive—and also developed a life-long fear of balloons.

* * *

August 1979, and the first day at school. Michael was happy to go and made a very special friend—Claudio from Chile. Claudio didn't speak English and had very big, dark eyes and black fuzzy hair, in contrast to my fair-haired little boy! Claudio and Michael were inseparable at school and playtimes saw them pretending to drive around the playground, using their hands as windscreen wipers!

I was able to understand Michael's speech, but it was a problem for the teacher and, in time, he started speech therapy. He carried out vocal exercises, but it wasn't working, so the speech therapist referred him to ENT (Ear, Nose and Throat). The ENT specialist concluded Michael should have his adenoids removed. The timing of this event coincided with us moving from Broughty Ferry to a brand-new house in Peebles—a fairly unsettled period in our lives, but a very fortuitous time.

Just after moving into our new home, the appointment for Michael's surgery arrived. We registered with a new medical practice and met our GP. I explained the situation and we decided to restart the process. An appointment was made to see ENT in our new hometown, and in time we met with this new specialist. He took one look inside Michael's mouth and immediately said that Michael must never have his adenoids removed as, in fact, he has a cleft palate covered by skin (I had been aware his uvula was split in two and was also very long). Removal of his adenoids would mean extremely impaired speech.

Somebody was looking after us! Indeed, we got great support from then on, with our fantastic GP referring Michael to Mr Brown at the Royal Hospital for Sick Children in Edinburgh. Mr Brown was a neurologist, and Michael would meet with him many times as he grew up.

At last, we were no longer on our own, someone was listening!

CHAPTER 2

From Birth to the End of Primary School – My Own Account

My poor mum had a very difficult time in the hospital. I was a very jaundiced baby, and I had two fingers fused together. My determination to get through health issues as a baby definitely showed I would be a fighter in life. My parents would 'wow' at every step I took towards a normal life; they expected it would be unlikely I would ever live an independent life and I would struggle with learning difficulties and challenges. Had it not been for my own determination, the great upbringing my parents gave me and the quality of schooling right from primary school, this would have been a more a likely outcome.

Obviously I don't have any memories of living in Newcastle upon Tyne, where I was born, given my family moved to a suburb of Dundee called Broughty Ferry when I was just a year old.

An early concern was my inability to walk at a normal age—as my Mum will already have highlighted, I could talk long before I could walk. While I'm sure it was exciting when I started to talk, it was very much a concern that I was unable to walk. I also need to apologise to my parents for my first word—car! Until my late twenties, I always wanted a job involving some kind of vehicle; in the early years, my ambition was to be a train driver, then towards the end of schooling, it was to be a car salesman.

Broughty Ferry was a nice place to grow up. I remember my first girlfriend at about the age of five, Jennifer, who lived nearby.

I was a very cute boy in early childhood—such blonde hair, and lots of it! Hard to believe now! I think I was often a bit shy, nervous and introverted.

We moved from Broughty Ferry when I was in about Primary Two. I really empathised with a Chilean lad called Claudio Agear (or something like that). He couldn't speak any English the whole time he was here—his dad was on an exchange year or something—but we were still able to communicate well. Randomly, he was fascinated with windscreen wipers, so we would bizarrely pretend to be cars in the playground, making the noise of windscreen wipers and using our hands as the wipers. It was really good fun—honestly!!!

Some funny early memories include: Me being quite upset and telling a passer-by, "My giraffe is stuck up the big tree!" A bendy plastic toy giraffe, of course. Me getting stuck in the bathroom and having to get rescued through the window by a neighbour, Murray. Playing on the bumper cars in the big park. Going to Fyvey's café for a juice while Mum had her coffee. Sledging on the "big" hill near the school—which actually, on nostalgia trips, was a tiny grass hump!

Even at a very early age, my clumsiness was there. I once ended up putting my wellies on the wrong feet and falling, resulting in splitting my head and causing a scar for life. This story is important, as that's an everyday task that I should have been capable of—this was more than just carelessness.

Another time my clumsiness affected me was at my friend's fourth birthday. I had been invited round to play football with the other boys, while his female friends played in the sandpit. He had proper goal nets, but I ended up getting so badly caught up in them that I was relegated to the sandpit with the girls—humiliation at such a young age!

Another clear memory is of my sister going to London to be on TVAM (now called GMTV) for the "Janitor of the Year" award. Our primary school janitor was the winner, and my sister's class got to be on TV. It was round about Christmas, and you got to see my sister watching Santa handing out the presents, but she ended up being about last to get one and seemed to be panicking that he might forget—although Carole should have known that Santa never forgets! She was really pleased with the doll she got.

Another memory was when Carole was on a school trip to Jersey. The night before she came home, Mum was out in Edinburgh with her friend, and a really, really weird thing happened. This was the mid-1980s, in the era before mobile phones. I woke up from my sleep in a panic and told Dad that Mum had been hurt in a car crash. About half an hour later, my mum called from the police station in Edinburgh to say she had hurt her neck in a crash. This was really freaky and a horrible thing; I can't really explain how I knew, but I guess there must be a little bit of psychic in me, and I've always had a close bond with my mum.

I can also remember, early-ish in life, coping with death. Mum's close friend Heather died of cancer and it wasn't easy for Heather's husband, Bill, or her kids, Claire and Brian, who were close family friends. Bill's mum helped bring Claire and Brian up, and she was an important part of our lives. I called her Gran Reid and, later in life, I went to see her in Elgin—both with Mum and then, soon before she died, on my own.

Another memory of Broughty Ferry was the neighbour's cat, Leo, getting run over, and me and my sister witnessing it. This was a horrific thing to see, especially as a young kid.

* * *

My dad is an accountant and worked for a textile factory in Dundee. He had done really well at a young age, becoming financial director or something similar. I remember my sister and I visiting the factory at a very young age and being fascinated by the fork-lift trucks and the (what felt like) huge space the factory occupied.

Dad's career was on the up, and he got a new job based in the Scottish Borders. We had to move home.

The process of house-hunting was great fun as a young kid, exploring potential new houses. Edinburgh was the initial likely option. I remember looking at a few places in Edinburgh, then South Queensferry, before we stumbled across the lovely border town of Peebles. We looked at a few interesting places around Peebles before coming across an amazing opportunity for my dad to buy land at the site of the old Langside Hotel and for us to get a bespoke bungalow built from scratch. As a young kid, it was always a great adventure for me and my sister to visit the building site and see the progress of the new house. I remember being fascinated with the foundations and also playing in the nearby wood, which went on for a good four hundred metres.

It was an exciting time, as was staying at my gran's big house in Bearsden near Glasgow after our old house was sold but our new house was not yet ready to move into. My gran had an amazing floored attic and me and my sister spent loads of time playing up there, out of the grown-ups' way. There was a spider that was always next to the loft hatch that looked like it had been dead for years. Once, I dared my sister to touch it, and when she bravely did, it started to move! Random childhood memory!

When the house was ready it was great. In 1982 it was such a modern house—still is to this day, to quite an extent. Sure, the bathroom colour schemes became dated—the main one was avocado, and my parents' en-suite was a pinky colour.

We had nice neighbours who, as a family, we got to know over the years. Some are still living on that street.

Some of my early Peebles memories involved me and my neighbour Andrew B setting up a five-a-side team called Langside Cuddy Rovers, along with Andrew D, Gary and Steven. We would typically play Elliot's Park Rovers and even Dean's United; participation was often an issue, sometimes it would end up being just me and Gary versus Dean! Andrew B went on to play football for a living, joining Leeds as a youth and ending up playing on loan for a Scandinavian team and then full-time with Clydebank towards the time they folded. He then ended up joining my favourite team, Dumbarton.

They wouldn't get away with it today, but back then, the old Kingsland Primary School had a small concrete climbing wall. Fall off that, and you'd land on a concrete playground floor! We survived, with a few bumps and scrapes here and there.

I can always remember, midway through my time in primary school, some musicians came in from outside the school. When they asked if anyone could play an instrument, I—much to my sister's horror—promptly and enthusiastically stuck my hand up, saying I could play the flute—something my sister went on to do very well! It was actually a penny whistle I got in my Christmas stocking, but Dad had said yes when I asked him if it was a flute! Whatever it was, I couldn't properly play it anyway. Glad I wasn't asked to give a performance!

I recall my now-friend inventing a nickname for me—dodo pie!—partly based on my clumsiness. Back then, school gates were open and folk used to take their dogs into the school grounds. The dogs would crap on the playground and, while we had an excellent janitor, he never could get rid of them all. The ones he didn't get were typically the ones I stood on. I just couldn't help myself—although it definitely wasn't deliberate!

I had a recent conversation with my friend, whom I never got on with at all at either primary or high school, despite having the same circle of friends at high school. I asked him for his views, as we now get on well, but he doesn't recall things the same way. I would say to an extent he bullied me. I also recall one occasion when I grassed him up for pushing or hitting me, but was disappointed and angry with my teacher's response, advising me not to tell tales!

We had a difficult teacher in Primary Three and Four— Miss A, who'd shout, scream, even throw rubbers at you—I don't even know if you actually had to misbehave to get this treatment! Anyway, one time, I recall her going into the walk-in cupboard to get stationery. The class joker locked her in for quite some time—how long exactly, I'm not sure. Seemed like ages and, from memory, perhaps some of the other teachers had selective hearing and were secretly quite happy. Collectively, the entire class took the blame, and nobody pointed the finger of blame at the class joker, even the swots! On another occasion, the same person didn't like his warm quarter-pint of milk and chucked it out the window, pelting our janny in the heid!

It was actually in this class that I had a funny turn that set me back until towards the end of high school—quite a frightening situation for my parents to cope with as well. I was, somewhat stupidly, swinging on my chair—perhaps partly due to boredom, stress and fear—and *bang!* I fell off and fainted, not sure for how long. I was taken to the doctors' and, from that point onwards, there were serious worries over my health in terms of potential childhood epilepsy. I had many EEGs and other tests; I was even overnight in hospital.

Towards the end of my primary schooling, I started to see a psychologist as well, in preparation for high school. The psychologist spoke to me about the chance of me being bullied at secondary school and gave me advice to keep in mind: the bullies were the ones with the problem.

* * *

One bad autumn, a big tree fell down in the woods next to our Langside Drive house. This was adjacent to our house but not close enough for there to be any risk. The roots came up almost like bars in a prison, but it had a fairly big hole.

The following summer, myself, my sister and Andy B did something cruel. I can't recall if the other kids involved, Michelle and Andrew D, saw it as a fun game or anything else, but certainly, on reflection, it wasn't good! We lured Michelle and Andrew to the uprooted tree as some sort of pretend prison cell, then me, Andy and my sister, Carole took turns guarding the prisoners! It was a very odd thing to do, but I don't recall any long-term fall-out with Michelle or Andrew.

Michelle's mum, Tricia, was actually a great influence. One of my unlikely achievements would be to ride a bike, and she essentially taught me one Sunday afternoon. Looking back and reflecting on my now-known dyspraxia, being able to ride a bike was a great achievement, and I think this helped implant the seeds of never saying "can't"! I'm not the best-balanced cyclist and am a bit wobbly; however, I'm pleased I can do it and quite like taking a bike around a cycle path. I can't really hand-signal, but when did you last see a cyclist do that!

* * *

I started to have some behavioural issues in late primary school and into the first three years of high school. My mum certainly feels a lot of this was down to my illnesses, the mystery, epilepsy-type thing, which possibly ties into my now-known dyspraxia, and my childhood brain damage. I would have some temper tantrums, perhaps akin to terrible twos, but I was nine or older.

One of my tantrums was, I believe, in my class in

Primary Seven. My teacher was Mrs Wilson, who was a great help and influence, and has now been Headmistress of Kingsland Primary School for a long time. I got so angry that I threw a chair at her. I never hurt her, but it must have been a worrying incident. She was aware of some of the issues I was having as there was good communication between her and my mum, and she dealt with me well. I was not really in trouble—in fact, her solution was to find more ways she could help me.

Much of this came from me being anxious about going to high school. There were some pre-induction days, but they seem to do the transition much better nowadays. When my sister's oldest two children made the move from primary to high school, they spent a lot more time at their new school in advance of the move.

One of the things that never helped me was knowing about the murders of children taking place not terribly far from Peebles. This was something I always had a fear of, possibly much more than most children. I remember my friend Scott recalling that he was on an organised Summer Club trip to Portobello Fairground the day Caroline Hogg was snatched and killed. I am certain I wasn't with him, but he thought I was.

There was another little girl from Coldstream who was sadly abducted and killed. The perpetrator ended up being caught in Stow, trying to abduct another little girl. I can always remember thinking that a man in a light blue Ford Escort was watching me and following me and I was always seeing his car; it was probably nothing, but I had an overactive imagination.

It was during this period of time, and then for a good five years or so, that I would have severe night traumas where I would be sleepwalking and sleep-talking. These would occur often, and I would sweat really badly; it would really freak my parents out. I would wander into the lounge absolutely dripping with sweat, claiming that I had been murdered! A really weird period of time.

I also recall that when I was asked to draw anything at school, I would often decide to draw a graveyard—not normal behaviour!

Our neighbour, Dr Wilson, would occasionally be called for when I got really bad. She was a brilliant senior nurse who wrote loads of books, some of which are still considered nursing bibles today. She would help with some medication I had been given for when I had these terrors. All these things were because of that fainting issue.

* * *

In terms of some of the happier times, I would enjoy Beltane through both my childhood and adulthood. This is Peebles' annual festival involving horses (the Riding of the Marches) and kids dressing up. There was a choose-your-own fancy dress; my first year was memorable for me being "Oor Wullie", a favourite comic book character—I honestly had the hair for it back then! For the main Saturday event, I would be allocated a costume. These included being a golliwog, sailor (for which I took an active part but was only just able to pull off what then seemed like tricky manoeuvres with a fake rifle), spaceman, elf and clown.

I can't recall if it was during Beltane or not, but it was definitely summertime. My mum was so worried as me and my sister had gone away for about half a day. We were only at the nearby caravan site playing but had clearly lost any concept of time. Mum had been phoning everyone. It was our family friend Douglas, who sadly is no longer with us, who found us safe and well. I think this was just about the only time we ended up grounded.

Carole and I got on well, but she was clever with how she played with me. She would enjoy playing with my things but made out that she never enjoyed things as much. She would always negotiate that if she played cars with me, in turn I had to help put on now-legendary plays with her. This involved me having to dress in her lilac leotard and leggings and do girly dancing. My parents and any friends round would have the pleasure of watching our creative visions while enjoying tasty homemade snacks such as mint biscuits (digestive biscuits spread with toothpaste)!

My sister's hero growing up was either Barry Manilow or my cousin Graeme! Graeme and Carole used to get up to all sorts of things, and I was usually the victim—persuading me to buy a "get out of jail free card" for £500 in Monopoly was a less sinister one. Knocking over my Aunt Betty's Christmas tree was a bad one!

My globophobia (fear of balloons) is somewhat unusual and was very much exploited by my cousin and sister. We all had open imaginations, and growing up in the technology-free late '70s and early '80s was a good time for just playing with basic things and using your imagination. So they told me about a ghost called Sparky, and the only way I would see him would be to drink water from a balloon, which was pretty much the worst thing you could ask me to do! I hated (in fact, I still do) every aspect of balloons—the look, touch and smell, more than just them bursting. Much to my disappointment and their amusement, after drinking from the balloon, I never saw the ghost.

I can cope with balloons and know it's not a rational fear, but I don't enjoy a meal if I'm even in the same room as a balloon, and if I'm choosing a restaurant by looking in the window, if there's a balloon there, I won't be eating there!

CHAPTER 3

High School Age

Moving to the big school was an exciting but very nervy time. I can remember our family friends, the Boags, were both teachers. When I asked Mr Boag how big the high school was, he gave me a talk about expectations, which was useful.

The summer before our first term at high school involved a really cool party where the three Peebles primary schools (Kingsland—my one, Priorsford and Halyrude) pupils were able to mix. Despite my dyspraxia—which was not known to me then but makes it harder for me to meet other people, particularly when it's loads of people—I seemed to really make the most of the new opportunities and had a number of new friends lined up for the first year at high school.

I was most nervous about finding my way around. The A4 paper map I was given on my first day was not easy for me to understand. The only boy from my primary school in my form class was someone I never got on with and, as mentioned in the previous chapter, we were more enemies than friends back then. This made it especially hard, as back in the primary school era of the early 1980s, boys played with boys and girls played with girls— not sure if it's still the same today, probably is.

I was quite lucky to have such a nice form

teacher. I remember the first thing he said after giving us his name was that he was seven foot tall, and I immediately replied, "No, you're not!" He was especially reassuring for my fears about getting lost. Almost all the teachers were really nice; even the ones I didn't like so much were respected by most people, with one or two exceptions.

* * *

Not surprisingly, subjects that involved motor/ practical skills, such as technical studies, which involved using drills and stuff, were a nightmare.

One of my new friends, Sammy—who was actually the Beltane Queen earlier that summer— looked after me in technical and home economics, although she essentially had to do her own task, then mine, so had to work twice as quickly. It was very sweet of her. We typically got away with this arrangement until she broke the drill one day. Obviously, it was my work being done, so I took the blame and got a bollocking—was the least I could do!

Sammy moved away fairly early in high school, but her mum is a friend of my dad, and I caught up with her socially in the late 1990s, which was great. Don't get me wrong—I would have probably broken the drill every time!

I was scared of anything like a drill or an iron – even to some extent a cooker – that had, for me, an element of real fear like heat or destruction. Home economics was a nightmare for me. Again, like Mr C in technical, the teachers of these subjects were less patient than most of the academic teachers. Mrs D was a nightmare for sewing and cooking—I was totally hopeless at both.

I can always remember a funny thing—and a really stupid thing, but again, coordination-related. I would get the manual kitchen scales, remove the measuring bit of the scales to put in the flour and butter and stuff, then notice the scales were reading wrongly (because I removed the measuring thing, which was quite heavy), so my measurements were always about twenty-five percent more than everyone else—a point that didn't go past the horrible teacher!

Music was the same. They attempted to teach us guitar and keyboard. I pretty much pretended to play these—especially the electronic keyboard. I would put the volume right down and normally change the instrument option from piano to saxophone, as you had all the buttons for different instruments. When the music teachers pushed the volume right up, a pretty hideous noise would come out!

I was good at singing, and late in primary school, I joined a Borders choir that the high school music teachers were in charge of. I had gone along to the church choir and, while nobody could deny I had a fairly good voice, my inability to stand up and sit down with perfect timing got me booted out! My parents were pretty angry. The deputy church minister, Rev. Lees, was very unhappy, as he had an ethos of the choir being available to anyone who wanted to be involved. He did everything he could to reinstate me, but the choir leader, who was also our high school music teacher, insisted everyone had to meet a minimum standard, which I never did because of my inability to stand and sit in total unison.

The one subject exception, on the more practical front, was PE. Despite my difficulties with coordination, my PE teachers were totally delighted with my participation and enthusiasm and were always full of praise for my efforts, which in turn made me enjoy the subject.

Other teachers that were good in early high school were Mrs McMillan for maths, Mr Moir for modern studies and Miss Dunlop for history (despite only doing history in first year). Mum was telling me recently that Miss Dunlop had asked about me, about fifteen years after she had taught me. I was well liked by most teachers and, despite my concentration not being good, I made every effort not to disrupt or distract the class. I was a very conscientious boy.

At parents' evening, it became obvious that I was not making the progress expected. Teachers, guidance staff, my parents and I were all in agreement about changing things a bit in second year.

I was allowed to drop some subjects, which was a relief in some ways—although I did miss history. To Miss Dunlop's credit, she had prepared some worksheets to make it easier for me; she did this just for me. I was sad to drop the subject, but I ended up choosing geography and modern studies instead.

I was delighted to drop technical and home economics and art—again, not all the art teachers were patient with me.

This gave me some free time at an early age, but I had to spend some of that time in the special learning unit.

* * *

It was mainly my friend Rod who encouraged me to join Borders Youth Theatre. I joined the year after my sister. Up until that point, there had only been two boys, Rod and Olly. My sister was ok with me joining; over the years, there have been many siblings who've joined at around the same time as each other. The theatre director, John, and one of the main organisers, Dave—who is Olly's dad— were both great influences and, to this day, I look forward to catching up with them every year or so.

The plays were a good discipline. I already had a little acting experience from Tweed Theatre Juniors, and also a little bit from the seniors in the annual pantomime, which I think I did twice.

The shows we put on at BYT (Borders Youth Theatre) were of a good standard, and this was a very valuable experience. I acted there for about six or seven years, as I did my final few shows after leaving high school.

An early sign of my dyslexia and dyspraxia was the fact that I couldn't easily remember my lines and would usually ask John to give me a bit part, something with no more than ten or so lines. Even at youth level, John trained us to a professional standard. He said if you forget your line, a prompt is amateur, so you need to improvise. This in itself set us up and helped with creativity. A number of our shows were created with the aid of improvisation. At occasional reunions, I have a lot of pride watching back through some of the old videos as the standard is that high. There is a bad one of *Salome* where most of the guys had to be ladies! I didn't enjoy wearing the red dress, but I seemed to play the part well!

Carole was more gutted than me when we missed *Thin Image*—a musical about anorexia— due to being in Sicily but, again to John's credit, on return from our holiday, we were able to be stage managers and move the set around in between scenes.

Many of the BYT folk have done well within theatre into adulthood. Sarah is an outstanding TV documentary writer, director and producer. My favourite work of hers was the Forth Road Bridge one. Halla is a news presenter for STV. Olly has gone on to direct BYT plays. Matthew and Colin have performed at the Edinburgh Fringe among other places.

Before going into sixth year at high school, I spent a summer with the Scottish Youth Theatre (SYT). It was good that Rod and Emma also attended that year, although we were all split into the three different groups.

This summer camp was a good introduction and preparation for becoming an adult. My personal hygiene was poor—I typically wore my SYT T-shirt unwashed almost every day—but it was here that I was, unbelievably, actually quite popular with the girls! It was at SYT that I put all my BYT learnings together and was brilliantly in character. Despite the usual bit-part requests, I managed to stay in character very well, even in the background, and actually won an "upstaging award". It was great to feel popular and feel I had accomplished something.

I stayed in touch with about eight or nine people for a few years afterwards. Stayed over at Lawrence and Gillian's house one Saturday night, wrote letters to David and Catherine, phoned Amy and met her for my eighteenth birthday. I wish had stayed in touch with Abby, who was very posh and shy, but we had got on so well. I remember her parents driving her home in a Rolls-Royce after our show!

* * *

Second year at high school was actually harder than first year. The clumsy way I walked, the way I talked, and even the unusual way I held my schoolbag made me a target for bullies. Some of the new first-year kids were crueller than my year, despite them being younger.

This was the start of five years of being bullied, right the way till the end of high school. I never really understood the meanings of the words, but a lot of the bullies would call me Gayfray and McMorton. The Gayfray one seemed to make out that I was gay, which I'm not, but I can see that I may have come across slightly camp. It was very hurtful, and I was not coping well at all.

This is one of my biggest criticisms of the school. I was fairly well schooled, but bullying should have been dealt with better. A few people would help me; my sister, Carole, was very good here, but generally you had to stand up for yourself back then. I suppose one of the positives was that it set you up with some life skills.

There were occasions where a group of us bullied my friend Tom. The group of us behaved badly and were really cruel and, looking back, I certainly regret it. I am not going to go into detail about the main incident—although I asked Tom a few years ago if I could mention it, and he was ok about it. I also had a couple of playground fights with Tom, one of which was broken up by a teacher. I am still really good friends with Tom and, to his credit, he is very forgiving. He left school at the first chance and went into farming. I visited him at the farm for a weekend and he let me drive the tractor, but I wasn't any good—somehow I managed to hit a fence!

Bullying wasn't just by pupils. Mrs E, who was actually a special unit teacher, was tasked to teach me touch-typing on a one-to-one basis. The school very kindly provided me with an electronic typewriter, which was a pretty advanced thing for the time, that I was able to use instead of having to manually write everything down. Mrs E was incredibly strict, and nasty and cruel. She would shout at my mistakes and, come the Easter holidays, she said I was way behind where I was meant to be and, as such, gave me what ended up being twenty-odd hours of practice. The threat of punishment meant I did this, meaning it was not a great Easter holiday. To date, I've never been able to gauge if this was meant as a punishment. I put pressure on my parents to deal with Mrs E and I was actually quite fast at two-finger typing. I think the dyspraxia meant that I was never going to be great at proper touch-typing.

Even though I had been at school for a while, I was only familiar with the rooms I knew. Mrs E sent me to get some books from another teacher, but I returned to the class terrified and empty-handed as I couldn't find the room. She thought I was lying about being lost and I had to spend twenty minutes at the end of the school day persuading her to give me my school bag back, missing my bus home.

Somewhat more tactfully, the fact I chose office studies in third and fourth year for Standard Grade meant that I could drop the typing anyway, which was such a relief!

* * *

Early in high school, my parents bought me what was then a state-of-the-art home PC—an Amstrad

464, complete with colour monitor. This was even before I was given the typewriter, and they had got a word processor and printer for it, meaning I was able to type and print some of my homework assignments anyway.

I would have the lads round often, playing a great Formula 1 manager game or *Brian Clough's Football Fortunes*, which was uniquely both a computer game and manual board game rolled into one!

We wouldn't always be on the computer; back then we would often kick a ball around. I still hung about with Steven and Andy B until I was in third year, so I had a good number of close friends. Subbuteo was another good thing, and we had a few good clubs set up in the high school. I was still a liability playing football. Even if Peebles Thistle were short of players, I would often still be a substitute. I never really took the hint just because I enjoyed it, but it really was a bit cruel!

I used to also go to Meadowbank running track, jogging with Steven and Andy, who were both good runners. I wasn't hopeless but wasn't fast. I was quite good at distance running—in fact, as a young lad, I did a 10k in around an hour, although Steven was a good ten minutes quicker than me.

As a family on a Sunday, we would go running with Peebles Hash House Harriers, through which we made many family friends, although my father left Mum towards the end of my high school days, having met his now-wife, Janice, through this club. We had many good Sundays jogging, following either a sawdust or flour trail, typically six-ish miles long, often for a few hours.

Dad had a sailing yacht called *Merle*. It slept four people and we had many adventures on board.

Again, my skills were limited to just steering. Dad was worried something would go wrong if I got involved in the other, more practical things such as putting up the sails, picking up a mooring or putting down the anchor. This reduced my enjoyment as I always wanted to try things, although steering was always good fun anyway.

Once we hit a rock, which was a scary thing; I was worried we would sink! Another time, when we got back from a trip to Inverkip Marina, my sister was allowed to take me out in the rubber dinghy, but only she was allowed to row. I liked rowing, and this was something I could do. Combined with the fact I was only allowed to steer under supervision on the main boat, I really wanted the freedom of being allowed to row the dinghy. I took the huff and told my sister I wanted to go back ashore, and she headed for the pontoon. I had started to get out too early and, before long, my body was forming a longer and longer bridge between the pontoon and the rowing boat…all of a sudden, *splash!* and Mum yelling, "He's in, he's in! He's in the water!" The water was the most disgusting thing you could imagine—very black and oily. Some other people helped me get out. We were only on a day trip this time, so I had no spare clothes. I ended up in my dad's waterproofs with nothing else at all to wear. My biggest concern, however, was that we wouldn't be going to the Kip Inn for an amazing fish and chip tea! We did still go there; I was a total sight and my mum a nervous wreck! I know Carole felt really bad—wasn't really her fault to be honest.

* * *

Despite my limited practical skills, one of my

favourite subjects was social and vocational skills—or soc and voc as it was known as. I was lucky to have lovely teachers, Mr Handyside and Miss Jack, who really looked out for me. I was hopeless at things like skiing but gave it a shot. My ski trip to Glenshee was mainly spent having coffee with one of the teachers in the café. I did try though, but had a bad experience with a button pull lift thing. I went flying off that—no injuries, but I was freaked out! I was also not great at running the playgroup; again my observational skills were not good enough at detecting if the kids were about to wet themselves. I enjoyed doing the playgroup and did get involved but just didn't quite have the skills.

In fourth year, I went to a driving centre in a wee automatic Austin Mini 850 and drove around the grounds. After that, they decided I would be ok to learn to drive without any restrictions when I reached seventeen years old, so I would be able to drive manual cars. This was a real relief for me as I always had a thing about cars—*car* being the first word I said! This news was also the start of me and my family starting to believe that I might survive in the big, bad world!

I had done ok in my Standard Grades to the extent that, for secretarial studies and modern studies, I was able to do the Highers in fifth year. I had great teachers for these subjects, Mrs Muirhead and Mrs Ritchie. Fifth and sixth year were good times, as we started the transformation into adulthood.

The school was split into four or five "houses", mainly for school sports, etc. I was actually vice-captain for Kingsmeadows. It was only me and Alan that put ourselves forward for this; he was a prefect, but I wasn't, so at least this gave me something to take pride in. Neither of us were that sporty and, while we would have both been happy to carry on these responsibilities into sixth year, our form teacher really pushed the sportier pupils into putting themselves forward in sixth year, so it was just for one year.

Into fifth and sixth year, things were looking up. The drama groups helped my confidence, my interest in politics really pushed me into achieving my Higher Modern studies, and my decent understanding of office practices and typing helped with secretarial studies. I had my exams scribed, which was really helpful, and the school really shone with their support—pretty good, especially considering this was the early 1990s!

In sixth year, I never really improved on my Highers but I had already pitched that I was going to do a HND at college and see if it would lead on to a degree. Sixth year was quite sociable as I only had a few subjects. Despite the lack of focus on the academic side, it was still an important year, preparing us for adulthood and maturity.

CHAPTER 4

Wild and Mad College Days!

My time as a seventeen-year-old involved a lot of changes: Dad leaving Mum, me passing my driving test. I was proud to pass a few weeks before my eighteenth birthday and also pass first time. I did have a fair few lessons and some additional practice in between lessons, mainly with Mum, at earlier times with Dad, and towards the test date, a friend of the family, Hugh, took me out a couple of times.

I was also about to leave home, at least on a Monday to Friday basis—I came home at the weekend on at least half of the weekends. It was strange and very exciting to leave home and move to the college. I think the short distance from Peebles to Galashiels was one of the biggest factors in my choice as I could be a bit insecure and homesick at times. The open day at the Scottish College of Textiles had been a great success. I felt it would be a friendly place to be and the Business Studies HND was an area I had done well at in school, studying similar subjects. My parents knew the course leader, Robbie, who assured me he would look out for me while at the college. It was nice to have a choice though.

I could have gone to Robert Gordon University in Aberdeen or Durham College to study hospitality management. I was really impressed by Robert Gordon, but my parents and I felt the practical nature of the hospitality industry would be tricky for me to manage. I also turned down a motor engineering course in Middlesbrough for similar reasons. I spent a good afternoon with a friendly course leader there, and I know he was disappointed with my decision as he had really low numbers and there was some doubt that the course would even have enough people to be viable. While I wanted to work with cars, I felt I'd struggle with being a mechanic. On reflection, I made the right decision, one hundred per cent.

I can remember the nervy, short journey to Galashiels with all my stuff, and the sad goodbye when Mum dropped me off. I knew she was only a phone call away (using the college's payphone as there were no mobiles back in the early 1990s, except for a few car phones).

I remember being welcomed by the friendly halls-of-residence reception team and being given the keys to my room, D2! I met my neighbour Phil, from Glasgow, who was doing some design course and seemed friendly enough. I also met lots of other folk who all seemed nice.

It was a good mix of courses from HNC computing, accounting and business to HND in the same, and a range of degrees in design and manufacturing through to honours and post-grad. I think my dad was really pleased with my choice as he was really senior in the textile industry. He must have been at director level from the late 1970s in Dundee right through to the end of his career. He had a successful career in what is a turbulent industry.

What was good about the serviced part of the

halls of residence is we got half-board, breakfast and dinner, and we also had a cleaner for the rooms. Mine really was a mess a lot of the time!

I was definitely a bit shy to begin with. I can't remember, but I probably had dinner on my own that night. I remember going to my room to watch TV; I even remember what I watched that Sunday night in 1992! It was a really good play about a female footballer who was so good she played for a men's team.

After breakfast the next day, I decided to go into town to look into getting a student bank account. It was a good thirty-minute walk, so I decided to get the bus; I had researched the time. A nervous-looking girl was also waiting for the bus. I sensed she was also a fresher (first year newbie) and thought it would be nice to chat to her. Her name was Corinna, and she too was going into town, mainly to open a bank account. We went to the bank together, then went for a few drinks. It was nice to make a new friend, as this had been a worry.

I think with my dyslexia and dyspraxia, friendship was not always easy. I don't like being in a big group—parties and big nights out can be tricky, or even approaching someone. Corinna was understanding. I think things could have been better with us, but I was a bit immature and was looking to quickly develop a relationship. We were always friends, but in the early days I think talking to other folk that I never knew well enough put paid to any romance and I felt bad for Corinna.

Freshers' week was all about social interaction and, at the freshers' fair, I looked to see what other groups to join. The Christian Union seemed like a good group with nice, like-minded people. This helped me socially, but two of the girls who signed me up were a bit mean to me a few days later and gave me a strong sign that they would be associates—part of the same club but not really friends.

I was also suspicious of a few cliques of people who constantly seemed to take the piss, mainly blokes. These were the people who were egging me on with Corinna. I think this made me a bit more insecure and I made a decision early on to be very wary of some people.

Through the Christian Union (CU) I was meeting generally like-minded people and am still in touch occasionally with a few folk, mainly through Facebook.

Eventually, with Mum and the CU's help, I decided to join my local Peebles church. I know that Mum and all my CU friends (and associates!) were proud of me doing this; most of the CU group were already church members. Other than for weddings and funerals, it was only during this period of time (1992-1994) that I went to church, mainly Peebles Parish Church but occasionally Galashiels Baptist Church (my present flat is opposite this church) and occasionally Charlotte Chapel, which is on Rose Street right in the centre of Edinburgh. The CU took me away from alcohol, which was no bad thing. I had a bit of a problem with alcohol as an eighteen-year-old—I would say I was a pisshead throughout my time at college.

A week or two into college I turned eighteen and me and my Peebles pals went to Fat Sam's. A friend, Amy, who I knew from Scottish Youth Theatre, met us in the Citrus Club a bit later. I hated that place, but it seemed to be the cool place to go back then! I fancied Amy and was pleased to meet her and introduce her to my friends.

I had a good circle of friends at college—my

closest ones were Bradley, Colin and Gavin. Out of these, I actually ended up being flatmates with Bradley and Gavin and was also at Bradley's wedding many years ago! On a Thursday, we would go into town at a horrible place called The Bizz. This was next to the cinema and, on student night, was either two-for-one or £1 a drink. We would drink quite a few, then head to the student union, where it was often £10 entry then unlimited drinks. All these things really encouraged binge-drinking.

Every now and again I would go out with other friends from the halls. The worst night we played a drinking game and I think I was a target. Everything was green that night. There was an awful cocktail called "green monster", then a French(?) Schnapps-type drink called Green Chateau?! Lethal stuff! This was the first really big night and there was a lot of challenging and daring each other to down our pints. Back at the halls, my room was spinning—never had that before—and (sorry, Mum and Dad!) I somehow threw up on the ceiling. The spew was dripping down on me the next morning, and I was feeling really, really immature and naïve, and this was very dangerous! I was lucky drinking never killed me. My sister got word of this—I think at the time I found it a bit funny (very wrong of me!) and I probably told her about the incident. Carole was furious with me but promised not to tell our parents. Back in the pre-social-media world, me and my sister would write to each other weekly/fortnightly, and we would even arrange to meet up via letter. She would stay at Mum's occasionally and have nights out with me either in Peebles or Galashiels, or I would have some great nights with her and her friends in Liverpool, where she was studying drama, art and English.

There were other nights where I was sort of showing off and poured an almost-full pint of stout over myself when showing off to the Irish girls; again, this was just really me being stupid. This was with another circle of friends. They would sometimes visit me at my dorm room or play pool with me. They kept on saying Caroline, one of the Irish girls, fancied me, but it was up to me to ask her out. I wasn't sure I wanted to go out with her and I was also not convinced this was not some further piss-take.

There was also a party I hosted when in second year. I had made my own homebrew—a pretty rancid beer that caused most people to throw up, but my stomach seemed to cope with it in small quantities! In second year, I was sharing a self-catering flat with other more mature folk: Jack (from Glasgow), Peter (from a posh part of England), Thomas (Germany) and Michael (Southampton). We all got on well and had a good party. My Peebles friends were over and my school friend Kevin had started a computer course and was actually in the year below me. I have followed quite similar career paths to Kevin. The party didn't end well as I foolishly never locked my bedroom door and some idiot poured a bottle of cider all over my bedding—never found out who did this.

Academically, and somewhat surprisingly, I was actually doing ok on the course. Not exceptional in any way, but I was more than managing. Between all the drinking, I was actually really good at attending all my lectures and tutorials. I always remember that one of our lecturers, Mr Kilgour, was raging as half the folk had skived his tutorial—a Friday morning tutorial after a big night was never a good thing. Mr Kilgour spotted me and I was genuinely not due at this tutorial! He asked me the rooms of everyone and, thinking how hilarious it would be to have him knocking on their doors, I told him!

Other friends, Frazer and David, would fart really loudly in some lectures, and the lecturers would have unimpressed expressions on their faces! I always found that sort of humour really funny. Also, there was one lecturer who was quite nervous and would say "mmm", "hummm" and "emm" a lot. We would take sweepstake bets on how many times he would do this in a lecture. Very juvenile stuff and I now applaud anyone who is able or tries to publicly speak—it can be daunting and, even if you do it often, it can still be scary, especially if the audience tries to take the piss. This was all mainly in first year; second year, I definitely took things more seriously, as did my peers.

In all seriousness the lecturers were very good, friendly and helpful. The smaller tutorial groups were a good opportunity to get extra help and understanding. There would often be assignments for these and I always did them, and ensuring I put in all the effort allowed me to achieve my HND. Generally, the subjects were really good and I had chosen the right course and college for me.

I was skint a lot, but what students weren't?! I chose to have a car and this cost me too much. I would always insure it, but a few times I was late taxing it and got a small fine. I couldn't really afford to have a car and shouldn't have had it. I had some wrecks as well! I have a short chapter dedicated to my cars so won't mention much about them here.

Some of my other good friends were Duncan and Roddy. They were the coolest guys you could get; they had real drive, even entrepreneurial spirt to them. They did things like buy a burger van and get permission to open it in the student union car park. They would make £100-plus every Thursday night. This was a lot of money, especially to students back in the early '90s! They also ran the pub quiz at the Golden Lion. Myself, Colin, Bradley, Gavin and sometimes Stu would have a team every week without fail. We were so like-minded to Roddy and Duncan, who thought up the questions themselves. They would not use quiz books but wrote the questions just from their knowledge. If we didn't win, we were second or third. Very rarely did we not win a prize! Quite a few times we would win the quiz and also win "best team name". We would think up a funny or topical team name every week, and again our sense of humour matched theirs totally.

I'm pretty sure that Duncan came to college straight from fifth year, so was always a bit younger than us. I can't remember if he left after the HND, but totally devastating was Duncan's untimely death, only a few months after his twenty-first. He and Roddy were in Liverpool and one of the best/worst things about Duncan was how sociable he was. My understanding was he was chatting to someone and they were just a thug and they shoved him to the ground. His head hit the concrete and he died in hospital hours later. Roddy very kindly called me just after the accident to warn me Duncan was not looking well and might not make it, then he called me again advising me of his death.

Things were never the same after Duncan died. I miss my college days and am only still in touch with a few people from them, which is sad. Through achieving my HND, I had the chance of staying on for a degree, but I had to decide whether it would be of value to me to stay on. I couldn't really afford to stay on, although I guess I would have got my dad's financial help to an extent. Leaving college made sense and getting an HND was a decent achievement.

I have often investigated doing a degree through distance learning—Open University, etc.—but I think it takes real discipline to do distance learning and keep the momentum going. Maybe sometime in the future? I was thinking of a degree in Politics. I have a chapter dedicated to the future, so will talk more about things there.

CHAPTER 5

Employment, Self-Employment and Unemployment in the Big, Bad World

I had not really had many jobs during school and college; in fact my earliest experience of a part-time job would have been when I was in my fourth or fifth year at high school. One of my friends, Grant or Hammy I think, helped get me a job at Peebles Hydro doing "kids' teas"—serving kids a meal, as the main dining was for the parents, so the kids generally ate earlier. This was a disaster of a job; my inability to serve food in a presentable style was another clue to my dyspraxia issues. One of my tasks was to spoon jelly onto plates—that was never going to work out! I remember rightly taking the blame for not hoovering well and the restaurant manager giving me a hand sweeper and suggesting I apologise to guests for not noticing I had missed some crumbs and food debris. This was humiliating, even at a young age.

A year or so later, towards the end of my time at high school—and much to my sister's horror—friends of the family, Janet and Alastair, who owned the Venlaw Castle Hotel, took pity on me and gave me a job in the evenings and some breakfast times. Again, though the will was there, I was pretty much hopeless, though always polite to any guests. I would sometimes wash the owners' cars, even take their dogs for a walk, then a bit of pot-scrubbing before graduating to the main restaurant. I was unable to carry more than two plates at a time—I never risked trying three! I was clumsy but can't recall ever smashing anything, though I struggled with stuff like being able to tell well when folk had finished. My politeness kept the guests sweet, and I just about got through it. My sister didn't really like being on the same shift but did tell me I wasn't the worst. Praise indeed!

I also ran the putting green/boat hire for three or four years. My friend Kevin's aunt, whom I previously met when I did work experience at the local council offices, let us run this. There was Scott, Kevin, me and, for the first year, Johnny. I think the second year was just me, Scott and Kev, and the next two years were putting only and just me. There were days where we only took home about 20p each but had great fun all the time kicking a ball around or having our own putting tournament for money—sometimes several times a day. There were also exceptional days where we made about £150 each. Overall it was a great way of getting through the summer and learning some business skills. It's a shame the facility has been closed for a good fifteen years now. The boats were knackered even when we had them; we used to rent them out with some of them having a slight hole in them but, back then, nobody would go too mad or threaten to sue! My hands got almost grated with the physical side of hauling the heavy boats up a steep bank, but I think the putting green would be a good wee business today!

My last season at the putting green finished suddenly. Having graduated from my college course, I decided to copy my friend Gary who, to this day, has only ever had one job, at Harrisons Ford garage in Peebles. I managed to secure an interview at another Borders Ford garage, where I think my enthusiasm shone through, although I suspect someone got the job ahead of me and never managed to get through the early months. My persistence—and a few chase-up calls saying I'd still not heard if I got the job or not—paid off when, all of a sudden, I got the amazing call saying I had secured the very job I had started to target following my college graduation.

I was so nervous the first day. Although I love driving, I was a fairly inexperienced driver. I was really worried about driving big cars and automatics, having never driven either.

My first day was a real challenge. The horrible senior salesman told me to come with him to the main Berwick garage, as this was the second branch. I was to pick up an automatic Montego estate and drive it back to Gala. I thought I was to wait on my colleague and follow him back, but no, apparently I was meant to have headed back right away. This was my first bad encounter with this bully. I got used to the car ok, though even a fairly new Montego was a heap of shit! My one had an overheating engine and I would see the temperature gauge going mad, then hear a hissing noise, but my colleague hadn't even let me follow him back—he was flat out in a V6 Mondeo from the outset. Somehow, I limped back in one piece and survived my first adventure!

It was Ian the sales manager who recruited me, along with Geoff the sales director. I also met the owner, Michael, and always got on with these guys. Ian soon jumped ship to an Edinburgh dealership, and then I heard the really bad news that George, the nasty salesman, was to take over. I was making steady progress, but the limited training I had had soon dried up more. The sales manager also seemed to want to take on more sales staff. I was making steady sales but was kept from getting involved in all the different areas of the business—generally, the sales manager would approve the trade-in valuations and the business manager would sort out the finance.

I think with proper support I would have done a lot better. My manager, in my opinion, had fly-by-night, double-glazing-type sales tactics, but essentially what he asked me to do was designed to ridicule me. He made me phone random people out of the phonebook and actually say, "I have a cryptic message that you need to see some lovely cars we have for sale." I certainly never made any sales through this; all it did was tarnish the brand. He was just humiliating me. I think I reacted to his bullying and ended up in a bit of a huff. He realised he had upset me, as he ended up following me to the café along from the garage one lunchtime. He apologised and said he would "learn me better". I hadn't been found to be dyslexic at this early stage, but this poor use of English made me chuckle slightly. Other dyspraxic tendencies included me several times asking if I could help two folk who were actually our company drivers/buyers. It took a good three or four occasions of me asking if I could help them before it clicked who they were!

Further humiliation took place and, despite my sales steadily improving, my boss told me he was interviewing people for my job. This was such a mean and disgusting move. I think he wanted me to quit there and then but I never did. He told me to act as reception and greet the candidates and offer them a coffee. I had a polite nature about me and complied with the instructions. He then decided to take two of them on and a week later he told me that this would be my last week.

I really pushed my performance and, on the Friday, he told me that as I was having a really good week, I could work both Saturday and Sunday and if I could sell five cars over those two days, I wouldn't be fired! This was not a realistic target, but I accepted the challenge and actually managed two sales on both the Saturday and Sunday, but in his office, he told me it wasn't enough and that I had failed the challenge. He held out his hand with a smug grin on his face and, while I never swore, I told him I wouldn't shake his hand. I knew he had a temper, but—evidence of his bullying— he told me he would beat me up unless I shook his hand. One of my regrets in life was giving in and shaking his hand. I would have absolutely got him done if he had attacked me; I wouldn't have retaliated. Sadly, he's still in the car sales world. I don't know if he's any different—I suspect he is. This was a really interesting experience, but a disappointing end to my first proper job. My car sales pal, Gary, met me at the pub and we stayed so late that my mum was a bit worried.

* * *

A very short period of unemployment followed. I think I was only out of work for a few weeks, then I went on a residential training course for an accident insurance company that did door-to-door sales. I loved the two-week residential training. We were very much looked after at a stunning countryside hotel in Wilmslow near Warrington. This leafy village was where loads of Premiership footballers had their mansions. The training was great fun, but a few months into the commission-only role, I was actually sometimes making a loss after the cost of my fuel was factored in; I can remember the finances being so grim that I ended up in tears at my dad's office—he was Managing Director at a Hawick textiles factory. He managed to sort out a medium-term arrangement with my bank. I think I quit the next day, and the benefits people gave me grief, threatening not to give me my benefits, but I reminded them it was them who really sold the job to me. A few folk were good at this job, but I was never all that comfortable with the script as it was very much slimy, door-to-door pressure sales techniques!

Again, I was only out of work for a week or two. I luckily managed to quickly sort out my first office job at an energy company in Gala. I was an admin assistant and very ordinary at it. I had lovely workmates here and was on a six-month contract. I needed a fair bit of help and support but was well liked and it was a nice environment. A few months in, they started to announce redundancies and, being on a temp contract, I was obviously told I wouldn't be staying beyond the six months.

I worked hard in the background and did well to secure an admin officer post at the Benefits Agency, although they couldn't give me a start date and said they would be in touch soon. True to their word, they were in touch saying it could be almost a year before they would get the admin office position, but I could accept an admin assistant position instead immediately. I was pleased with this, although even back in the mid-1990s the starting salary of £6700 was really poor! I was particularly pleased to have avoided a further short spell out of work by going from one job to the next. Back in this time, all the companies had a lengthy paper application form on top of the CV—technology these days makes applying for jobs so much easier.

During this time at the new permanent job, I felt much more stable and actually bought my first flat, a one-and-a-half-bedroom place in Earl Street, Hawick, the half room being a box room. The flat was a bargain at £13,000 and I bought it furnished from a minister's son. The bed was even made when I arrived to collect the keys!

This flat really set me up and I was the first person in my circle of friends to get their own mortgaged place.

I never really met many people in Hawick but was never too far from Galashiels or Peebles. My dad stayed in Hawick, and his wife is an exceptional cook. I would go for a meal roughly once a week, which was good.

My job was really basic, I would spend the mornings filing and the afternoons handwriting giro cheques. It was repetitive and boring—again I was liked but mediocre at it. I remember a mistake: I once posted a giro cheque made out to "Mickey

Mouse". I had no recollection of this and must have been in a trancelike dream for it. I guess my very poor handwriting was just about acceptable.

My appraisal was fair: "Jack of all trades but master of none"! The big boss there took a shine to me and put me on the amazing vocational scheme, the Prince's Trust. I was going to spend about six months full-time learning life skills, adventures, teamwork and residential stuff. It was a very kind opportunity and I was privileged to have been invited to it—many of my colleagues were a bit jealous. I had gone to a few sessions, meeting other Benefits Agency employees from other Scottish offices who I would be doing the scheme with. It was really exciting, but I soon had a real dilemma.

My heart still leaned towards getting back into the motor trade and my luck was in when I saw a job advertised at the local Rover/LDV van garage in Galashiels. I did well in the first interview and was invited for a second interview, essentially to ask me another few things and offer me the job there and then. I couldn't refuse, as it was what I wanted to do. With some sadness, I turned down the outward-bound opportunity, although it was a relief to finish up at the Benefits Agency—it was so boring and repetitive.

With my new job, I worked closely with Alastair, the sales manager. It was just me and him and he taught me well, showing me how to value cars and even buy stock. He trusted me, and I was able to soon make some good sales myself. I even had my own office. It was cool but quite old-fashioned; this was back in the day when people smoked in their offices! I had an ashtray but never used it!

My sales generally improved month on month. I got on great with Alastair. I was ten months in, with a company car or even occasionally a company van and sometimes a tipper truck! I was well paid and had cleared all my student debt and was in good shape financially, but I was nervous, as I had never managed to hold a job for a year!

When things were going so well, suddenly my world was brought crashing down when I was told that my boss's pal had his eyes on my job. He wanted to stop being a motor trader and take over my role. I was pulled into the managing director's office and was told that Neil was too much of a talent and he would get my job.

I felt very let down. While I was not doing exceptionally, I was a fairly young guy— twenty-two years old, if I recall the timing—and getting better all the time. I decided the world of the motor industry was too cutthroat, and I also accepted I was not a talent, just ok. I would not take such a risky job in the near future.

* * *

It was slightly harder to get my next job. This was in the summer of 1997 and I was in a bit of a downer. I was worried about how companies would feel about all the job changes I'd had. The job centre was horrible. At a signing-on session towards the end of my unemployment they threatened to withdraw my benefits as I had not applied for any new jobs that week. I told them this was due to having five interviews, which had taken six weeks or so to get, and I was sure I would get an offer. I ended up getting two offers—an insurance company in Glasgow, which seemed like a good job but would be disruptive as I couldn't do the commute from Hawick, and a large energy company in Edinburgh, which was do-able although quite a commute.

I opted for the energy company. This was also my first call centre job; I was determined just to get my head down and get through my first year. I really was concerned about my ability to last in a job although, all things said, I've only had two jobs that I was fired from—both the car sales ones. The training was amazing, totally different from all the other companies I'd worked for. The call centre felt huge; I had only ever worked in the Borders up until this point, so it felt strange working in such a big place. I was a bit slower than most of my peers but made steady progress. We were quite a big group, about twenty of us. My co-workers were nice, and we all stayed together after training, with a few more-experienced team members to give us a bit of extra help and support.

A full year passed and, unusually, I actually celebrated my anniversary, such was the achievement. A number of folks from the group had left, but I was doing quite well. As well as that, I was told I was now permanent, and these were the days of a formal paper contract. This formalisation was actually an enjoyable part and felt part of the achievement. They told me I had done well.

The additional security had a positive impact on me esteem-wise and I suddenly announced to my family that I had secured a place to run the London Marathon! Everyone was delighted for me. I got a charity place with "The Princess of Wales Trust"—she had died the year before in the Paris car crash. My sister, Carole, came down to London with me and, when I arrived just outside Earl's Court to get my number, I saw our team captain, Paul Burrell, who had worked for Princess Diana, approaching from the other direction. It felt really weird, as if we both knew each other, as he was sort of waving at me. He had a nice chat with me and was delighted that I was running in his team. I ended up catching up with him and Chris Moon, who was a para-athlete who had lost an arm and a leg in a landmine accident.

My team had previously put me in touch with Anna from Melrose, as she had asked the team if there was anyone local she could jog with. We had met every Sunday and raised the length of our runs up to about fifteen miles. This included doing the Clackmannanshire half-marathon, which was quite hilly; Anna did well with this, but I struggled and was one of the last to finish, so I was beginning to panic a little.

Anna was a great support, and we had become good friends. Her sister, Lisa, had also come down to London. Anna agreed that we would start the marathon together and see what happened.

One of my regrets in life—a fairly trivial one, all things said—was that about seventeen miles in she wanted to drop the pace a bit and such was my stamina that I actually wanted to increase the pace and try to get a better time. On reflection, I really don't think this was the right thing to do!

I think I had predicted a time of six hours, but in fact I crossed the finish line in almost exactly five hours and thirty. My sister had watched me finish, along with Anna's sister, Lisa, who was panicking a bit that her sister wasn't there but understood my reasons for pushing ahead and that Anna wouldn't be too long. I think she came in around the targeted time of six hours.

We all went to the post-marathon team party. Interestingly, Chris Moon, who only had one arm and leg, had got a time of about four hours! His next challenge was the Sahara Marathon, running 26.1 miles in around 120 degrees Fahrenheit! I think I'll give that one a miss!

This was just a drinks party, so my sister and I decided to go for an Indian meal. Anna and Lisa declined to join us. After the meal, a really funny thing happened—I couldn't actually move, my legs had turned to jelly. I wasn't scared or anything, it was just a hilarious sensation. With my sister's help, I managed to stagger back to the hotel. I was actually right as rain the next day and felt amazing, although my post-marathon shower was pretty brutal as I had bleeding nipples! There is photo evidence!

Anna never really forgave me, and I can understand. We never stayed in touch. It was a selfish move from me, and I have certainly learnt from this.

I actually did the London Marathon again the following year. I didn't train much and now appreciate that this was stupid and a bit dangerous. My choice of charity was a bit selfish. I went with Get Kids Going, lured by the incentive of a free Concorde flight as I got my place through the ballot should I make £1500-plus for the charity, which I did. It was so competitive for the charities back then that such incentives were there. Tragically, the Air France Paris Concorde disaster happened, so I never ended up getting my free flight.

Anyway, back to my work. Now I was doing well enough to be added to the floorwalking pool and was helping new starters. Eighteen months in, team leader jobs came up. I had an almost one-hundred-percent interview success rate so far in life—I think back then, not really knowing about some of the learning difficulties I had, I seemed to be much more confident and was great at interviews. I asked my then-TL, Lindsay, for some advice and she gave me amazing pointers. I ended up not only getting the job but also being told I had the highest points tally out of all the candidates. Without a doubt, I wouldn't have done so well without her coaching—not sure if I would have got the job or not. This was bittersweet for Lindsay as her friend Fiona didn't get the role. It seemed a bit embarrassing and she seemed unhappy I had got it ahead of her friend; it was quite a competitive environment. I was, however, over the moon.

Life as a TL was great. My boss, Graham, told me I was totally first pick and he had sounded out some people about me. The structure then was a team manager with two TLs, and then a fairly large team of about twenty or more customer services advisors.

The TL role was pretty much being delegated tasks from the Team Manager, being second in command. The other newly appointed TL was Peter, who actually started at the same time as me. It was a great achievement for us both, having got our first promotion after only eighteen months. We made a great team—I loved Peter's humour and wit. Graham was a great boss, we always got on well and I really grafted for him, did loads of quality monitoring and was like the team expert—helping make decisions with tricky accounts, taking over escalated calls, running the team when Graham was on holiday, etc.

I can recall a great team night out when we went to a thing at the Edinburgh Fringe called Late and Live. This was mainly up-and-coming stand-ups. The show started about midnight, but there was all sorts going on until about four in the morning—not that I stayed that late! I remember one of the up-and-coming new talents was Johnny Vegas and, to the delight of the team—and embarrassment of me—I was the person in the audience that Johnny decided to pick on! It was funny, looking back!

Back then, there was a company awards presentation around Christmastime. I was a bit suspicious as loads of people kept asking if I would be going along—yes, I would tell everyone! Turns out I was to be given the award of Special Contribution by a company director, which was essentially the main award. There was such a flattering speech by one of the senior managers, in which he likened some examples of my helping people to Jesus! I think he took the praise too far, but I was totally over the moon!

I wasn't always Mr Nice Guy, and a difficult situation had recently happened. I had caught Peter's girlfriend deliberately hanging up on people. I discussed it with Peter first and he agreed that I should do the right thing and not turn a blind eye—not easy for him. It was agreed he would not get involved and Graham wanted to see how I coped, so I was essentially tasked with sacking the girl. The conversation was difficult, but while she initially denied it, I had pre-empted that and was able to play the calls that proved it. The HR department helped with the formalities after that. It was a lot easier to do these things back then; nowadays, and quite rightly too, there are much more robust disciplinary procedures to follow that give more protection to the employees.

Soon after this, my manager Graham advised us he had got a great promotion as a business analyst but was having to move to London. My sidekick, Peter, then got a sideways move to the resource management team. Graham told me he had convinced the senior management team that, if I wanted, I could take over as team manager on an "acting up" basis. Everyone was delighted for me; the team got on with me. I was a bit nervous about having my own team leaders, and would I be able to delegate well?

My team were generally really young and most of them had been recruited onto a shift they never liked, twelve noon to 8 p.m. Due to expansion, one of the other challenges for us all was hot-desking. There were not enough desks, which meant that we were scattered everywhere. Morale was low, but there were no easy solutions.

It didn't help that I had to sack someone else for threatening a customer. I actually just stumbled across the call through random call listening remotely and, to my management credit, I had previously identified and coached the same individual on his weaknesses when dealing with conflict. There was supporting evidence of a decent coaching history, and there was no excuse for him doing this. Two of the senior managers actually visited the customer with a bunch of flowers and a bottle of wine. Again, I was fed back a lot of praise for dealing with this well—wasn't at all easy!

I came up with some suggestions for the hot-desking issues myself, but there was only really one proper solution. It worried me—selfishly, because I was only acting up on a temporary basis—but disbanding the team was inevitable. The senior management team had been delighted with me and actually offered me the job permanently in the twilight department. This was almost a case-study scenario as I never had to go through another interview—this was known as succession planning, but while it was quite controversial, it was fair as I had really served my apprenticeship!

I was very nervous moving to twilight, which was the 2 p.m. to 10 p.m. shift, as the nature of the job was quite different. I was to take a non-telephone processing team known as CPP, and the team hadn't yet been recruited. This was really interesting, as it involved me going on a business trip to our Manchester office because the work was being migrated from there. I faced a lot of resistance there, as there was resentment that the work was being taken away from that location. It was a frustrating week and I probably should have learnt more on the business trip than I had, which made it trickier.

I was involved in recruiting half my new team. This ended up being a nightmare scenario and a big mistake by my employer. They made the decision to directly employ half the staff and get the remaining half via the recruitment agency on a temporary-permanent basis. This created a huge divide within the team as some had financial security and a higher salary. I never managed this well, although it was a hopeless task. My manager held a meeting with the team but not me—essentially a vote of confidence. Apart from communicating better and more honestly to folk, I'm not sure what I could have done. It was a nightmare of a situation and not fair to me as a fairly rookie manager! I actually felt like quitting. This was my first real setback since becoming a permanent manager, but I survived and got through it.

Adding to this, one of the team resigned soon after and wrote quite a nasty letter about their experience, highly criticising me as manager. While my boss had backed me up and I wasn't in any bother, I felt I lacked enough support as a rookie manager.

Things soon got a lot better; I worked hard at regaining the team's trust. The new type of work was challenging and not without hiccups, as we were all new to it. We were constantly learning through experience and things were starting to work a bit better.

My number one aim with the team was getting people their contracts, as long as they worked hard for them, and I gave loads of extra help and support. I definitely went over and above. Soon, I had the team in as good of shape as possible.

I had a number of different TLs through this period. One asked to move from the team, due to the other TLs being part-time and her being full-time. She felt the part-timers had not pulled their weight. It was quite dramatic and again another setback.

One of the new TLs I got was Anne, who became a good friend. She told me, as an older member of staff, that had it not been for me encouraging her to go for promotion, she would have just carried on doing the entry-level customer service advisor role.

Anne went on to become a manager herself. She said working for me had been amazing and that she had learned so much. I was so proud to hear that in her new role at one of our other Scottish offices she had gone on to get a one-hundred-percent feedback score from her entire team in a whole employee satisfaction survey, which had never happened before! She received an award at a national event, but told me again that I was the main influence on her management style. I was so flattered!

I had come through the issues and my team had

settled down and, like in my old TL days, I was more respected and highly thought of again.

* * *

Another exciting thing that happened was I bought another flat! I couldn't sell my Hawick flat, but the mortgage was so low that I just rented it out, which was a lot easier than selling it.

I was really lucky with the new flat. It was a brand-new place. When I first went to the show house, they told me that the entire development had sold out, as people had actually camped outside for several nights, but they could put me on a waiting list. This was subject to me getting onto the council housing waiting list, which I was eligible for back then due to living a certain mileage away from my place of work. It's probably harder to get on these days!

Bizarrely, despite being low priority on the council housing waiting list, I was actually offered a flat in Oxgangs. I think it was a situation where, if I didn't accept the property, I would be removed from the list, although I had already given Wimpy Homes—who were building the new flat—the proof I was on the list.

I shortly got the good news—for me—that loads of people had struggled to get mortgages, and I was asked if I wanted to buy a one-bedroom flat in the regeneration of Muirhouse. This was not the nicest of areas and was a slight risk, but it was a really good feeling to secure a one-bedroom flat for just £27,000! This was about a twenty-minute walk or five-minute drive to work, so was very handy! I spent a very good seven years or so there.

* * *

After a few years running the twilight team, I politely asked about getting a more normal daytime shift, allowing me to improve my lifestyle. My manager and also their manager agreed that I had served my time there and said they would have a think about other opportunities.

This led to my most enjoyable year with the company. Essentially, I was to be involved in a couple of outsourcing opportunities. The first one was in Leicester, and it was actually migrating some of the work I went down to Manchester to learn about. This was not plain sailing, but I really enjoyed the adventure. I did this for around ten weeks. I was reporting to Les, who was a lovely fellow, very funny but always full of praise and accepting of my judgement.

I had been assigned two people to support this project. I didn't have a say in choosing them and knew that one of them could be hard work. This was totally the case. She was constantly criticising me, the processes and everything else. The new agency staff doing the work were nice folk and got on well with me. While I enjoyed the experience, I was glad to an extent when the ten weeks were up. My manager told me he was happy with how things had gone.

My next challenge was just amazing and possibly one of the best things I did in my time as a manager. It was to create a training plan for new starters who were going to be part-time, working from six to ten in the evening, taking calls between six and eight and then doing processing work until ten. I cooperated with the daytime training team and took copies of their training folder and PowerPoint presentations, which I then tweaked for the new folk. I spent a few weeks doing the classroom side, which I loved the most, then after that we had a development zone where the new starts would take calls in a strongly supported environment.

I was able to pick my own floorwalkers to support me and had an amazing team. Two of the team have gone on to great things away from the utility industry. Esther is very senior in a maritime role with saving sharks in South Africa—I believe she has done a lot of practical research about the great white! Callum, whom I catch up with almost annually, is about second-in-command at a CV-checking service in Cyprus. He has also told me that he could sort me out with a job if I ever fancy moving over to Cyprus. It is very tempting, but I will see how the next few years go in the meantime!

My next assignment was running a satellite operation in Glasgow. I was incredibly nervous as I was essentially in charge at the location but had a manager who would be based in our Edinburgh office. The work the staff did was quite basic; this really suited me as I never liked dealing with too complex situations, although generally I was quite good at problem-solving. Unfortunately, this opportunity was plagued with telephone issues that caused customers to be cut off, and there were no reassurances that issues would be resolved quickly; as a result, the plug was pulled after about four weeks.

On returning to Edinburgh, I was told I would be running two different teams in tandem. One of my teams would replicate what I had just done, and the other was our admin team. This team was made up of people who either never liked telephone roles or were unable to take customer calls due to disabilities/learning needs, etc. They dealt with things like faxing forms, sending out meter box keys and clearing answer-machine messages. This was a lovely team to run and again, on reflection, suited my own still-undiagnosed dyspraxia/dyslexia by being a fairly straightforward function.

The biggest challenge was that we needed more people to do the basic phone function. I was to help assess who could/wanted to take these calls from the admin people. It was a tough thing, as some of the team wanted to take the calls but, due to speech impediments or other issues, would have had customers unable to understand them easily. Many of the team hated this and some were so scared. I essentially held their hands through this and did a lot of demonstrating and reassuring and praising their efforts.

I felt really bad but, about nine months down the line, I applied for a job in the Leeds office as a department manager on a seconded basis, and I actually got the job! I had worked incredibly hard preparing answers for what I expected the interview questions to be. It helped that I had been involved in a lot of recruitment activities and I totally nailed the interview. I'm not sure if I did quite as well in the other parts of the assessment, but this was a great achievement and to date is the highest position I've been employed in.

* * *

I was really pleased, but the role was predictive-dialler departmental manager. It was a very technical role; clearly all the applicants had a fairly limited experience of dialler, as I had got the job with no experience, although when I got my interview letter, I arranged through one of my pals that ran a dialler team in Edinburgh to listen in and get an understanding of how it worked. I think this helped me get the role.

The people-side went really well, but the harsh reality was that I was so out of my comfort zone and a little homesick, it just wasn't going to work. About four months into my six-month secondment, my manager, Sarah, was good about how things were progressing and told me she was more than happy to keep going for the next two months and then see if I was close enough to take the role permanently. Alternatively, she offered me a team manager substantive role there, and let me know that I could just return to Edinburgh if I wanted. I apologised that I had not done better and told her I would prefer to return to Edinburgh. She was so nice about everything and told me she thought I was doing ok, especially with the people side of things.

Back in Edinburgh, the timing was good. One of the team managers was moving to project work and I was able to slot in and take over the team. It was a fairly new team; things went well until my manager, Robert, got promoted himself and Karen took over. She was a cross-the-T's and dot-the-I's sort of person who wanted a level of detail that I found really hard to consistently deliver. There were really high expectations about the number of call-listens and that sort of thing to do. I was put on action plans for my time management and criticised severely for my organisational skills.

I actually ended up off sick for about four weeks due to stress, which was the longest time I had been off any job, but I was feeling pretty low. Things were a little better after I took this time off.

My manager firmly told me I was to go onto a residential training course in two one-week parts. I got the impression she meant for this to feel like a punishment, but secretly I was totally delighted. I had worked with Karen previously and we had got on really well, so it was a shame I didn't get along with her as a manager. On reflection, I'm sure she had my best interests at heart but was frustrated that I was unable to match her levels of detail.

After about a year there was a restructure and I ended up reporting to her manager, Paul, who seemed to empathise with me more and helped me tweak some of my time-management techniques. Soon he was describing me as one of his strongest managers. He was realigning some of the teams and proposed to use me as a spare to cover the other managers for annual leave and sickness, but when a vacancy came up at complaints, he identified this as a real skillset of mine and thought I would be best placed to run the complaints team. I wasn't overly keen, but I knew it was what the senior management team wanted me to do, so I went along with it.

I found it a tough job, it was a difficult team to manage, and I felt a lot of the team took their frustrations at difficult calls out on me. It was exactly what I'd expected. I never liked it; it was a more heated department to work in, and my personality was not right for that.

* * *

During this time, I had managed to get hold of a "golden ticket", which was a promotion by KitKat and Channel 4 for the popular TV show *Big Brother*. It was an amazing experience; I was put up in a suite at a nice Central London hotel and went through extensive screening. Also, my friends, family and employers were called by the *Big Brother* production team. My poor mum was trying to enjoy a holiday abroad but was pestered by Channel 4 researchers two or three times.

My then-boss actually arranged a sabbatical retrospectively in case I did get on the programme. He also contacted a former contestant who still works for the company.

Despite my boss being helpful with the sabbatical, he had been quite critical of me and told the producers that he didn't think I would cope too well. Also, my dad had some reservations.

The psychological tests were mainly where I fell down. The psychologist had been drawing shapes and things when I had been chatting to him and doing some tests. I didn't understand the meaning of these. Around a third of the ticket holders never made it onto the live golden ticket show, so at least it wasn't just me. I did enjoy the process but was probably too honest with the producers, who had told us to be fully honest with them! And I did enjoy the hotel suite. The hotel was very much a three-star, but I must have ended up in one of the nicest rooms, which added to the experience.

* * *

I had been tentatively looking at some alternative careers, as I didn't want to be stuck in complaints, with or without getting through some sort of performance plan. On asking to move departments, my boss, Dave, initially said that would be fine, then a week later he told me out of nowhere that I was vastly under-performing! Choosing to exit a decent salaried role was a difficult decision, but I felt I really needed the change. This ended my nine-year stint there.

I had looked at a number of unrealistic "get rich quick" schemes, which mainly involved some pyramid structure, and I sussed that these were things to avoid, but an American estate agency caught my eye.

I went to a seminar and had a meeting with the recruitment chap, and it seemed like a risk worth taking. Rather than rushing into anything, I thought a bit more about things over the next few weeks. It was a big decision as I would be leaving a decent level in a secure, large organisation for self-employment. Was I motivated enough to get up and look to make money? It was not going to be some cushy number where I could just hang around waiting for the phone to ring. They had all the American marketing techniques, which probably don't work as well today as they did ten or fifteen years ago. A lot of it was marketing cards, and there was an expectation you would deliver by hand at least two hundred of these a day, especially on the back of listing a property on the market.

I discussed what branch to join in Edinburgh, and the Leith Walk one seemed to meet my needs. I was probably expecting more support for my monthly fee; this was almost like renting a desk at a hairdresser. There were not enough desks, and when the established agents arrived at the office on my first day, I was booted out for the rest of the day as, rightly, they needed the desks.

My training was great fun and the flamboyant Scotland franchise holder, a likeable Canadian fellow, was quite hands-on and made a point of getting to know all the agents. At the peak, there were a good few hundred of us, with around a hundred offices and shops in Scotland.

The downside to my training was that there were three of us there from my office—they should have a rule that only one person from the office went on the new-start training. A more outgoing person— Shane from Orkney—was a better, more natural networker than me, and he ended up getting more referrals. There was a referral system for if one of the folks from the other office knew someone looking to buy or sell in our area, where you shared the profits. This worked well, and I did do some referral deals, both passed my way and on to others. I had a few deals that never paid my share as well!

I tried to think outside the box and Gumtree was the big thing then. We were taught how to market "for sale by owners"—people trying to sell off-market. A big company, who are now even bigger, were impressed with me unwittingly targeting some of their properties, and I was called into a meeting with the managing director. I forged a relationship during the three years or so I was in estate agency and got some properties to sell. I also took advantage of my last employer and managed to get into their workplace, inviting a solicitor and a mortgage broker to join me, and the three of us got a lot of deals. On one visit alone, I ended up listing four properties that, combined, sold for almost £500,000! I had referral schemes and gave bottles of wine and chocolates just for listing a property with me.

The role was great fun, and it was a skill to be able to accurately value and market a property. I was impressed with my coordination and accuracy and was proud I was able to do a professional job. I can't really ever recall a complaint. We did Saturday half-day rotas on running the shop, just answering calls and that sort of thing. A lovely Polish lass—Yolanda—called in a few times, and she sort of asked me out. While she was never my girlfriend, we had half-a-dozen or so coffees and drinks, and it was great to catch up with her.

The first year had gone to plan, I was doing ok, but I sniffed that the credit crunch was about to happen—there were some indicators of the changing tide. I decided to profit from my own place. I sold my flat in Muirhouse, Edinburgh, which I had bought for £27,000. I sold it for a record £100,000, which I don't think has ever been beaten by any of the new builds in that development. I had bought and sold at the right time.

I decided to move to Dumbarton and actually managed to pay cash for my three-bedroom flat, which had an amazing view of the Clyde. As well as buying my flat, I also spoke to the owner of the Alexandria branch of the estate agency, who was happy for me to join his branch, although he pre-warned me he was likely to exit the franchise soon. We enjoyed working together, and he was a likeable fellow, but it was a tough market and I only achieved a few deals there. Before long, he closed the office.

I then moved to the Paisley office and didn't do all that much better. I've stayed friends with Diane, who was a joint owner of the office, to this day. In fact, she is the only person I'm really still in touch with from my estate agency days.

One of the challenges of working as an estate agent was keeping up with laws and rules. Scotland has had a number of new rules regarding property and I think I would find it overwhelming today. I think that I have a limited capacity with my disability and I can reach a limit and want to just forget about it all when it gets too much.

I actually kept the estate agency going part-time when I got my next two jobs. My next job was with another energy company, doing door-to-door sales. I had gone through a recruitment company, who were excellent in preparing me for the interview. I think I saw this as a chance to top up my money. From memory, there was a joining reward of around £1500 after the first month or two and I also had a company car—some six-speed Fiat, something Turbo, and it fair flew!

Training was in Nottingham and was great fun, although I was burgled the day before. The local police were disinterested, and they never even reported the correct stuff stolen to the local press. I was in a rough part of Dumbarton, and I decided that I'd had enough there. I was disappointed about how living in Dumbarton had gone; I had some good friends there, but it was really the flat—it would have been fine if the neighbours hadn't been a bit dodgy. There were drug dealers and addicts in my stair, who were desperate and attracted more dodgy people.

I had a client who liked to buy that sort of place and, believe it or not, one fifteen-minute phone call to her and I had sold my flat for what I paid for it—and bear in mind I'd never had a mortgage payment to make! I had made some useful connections within property, mainly buy-to-let investors. Looking on Zoopla, I can see she still has this flat, so it must have worked out well for her. I enjoyed a great company conference in Blackpool. I always remember how stormy it was, and there was a bit of a hairy coach trip from Glasgow. We passed several overturned lorries on the way down, and right outside the hotel was the Heysham (England)–Warrenpoint (N. Ireland) ferry in trouble, having been beached. It was just a small ferry that looked more like a small cargo ship—I think it had eight lorries on board, and everyone was ok.

I was staying at Norbreck Castle, and it was a good, fun event. That's something I miss from sales roles—the motivational conferences. I only stayed three or four months in this role and it wasn't great. I was sometimes nervous door-knocking—it's a tough reception, and in the ten years since, it's become unacceptable for companies to operate door-to-door and rightly so. It was salary-plus-commission though, so the money side was actually pretty decent!

* * *

I only left this company after landing what is definitely my favourite job that I will probably ever have, which was for a long-haul tour operator in Glasgow. My clients were all travel agents and I really enjoyed my interview. On joining up, my interviewers, Caroline and Jennifer, often talked fondly of my interview, full of enthusiasm. I had got the travel bug only a few years before this, but I will document my travel experiences in separate chapters.

I was trained as an Australia/New Zealand/round-the-world expert. The training was such fun and exciting. Helping plan round-the-world trips was a great experience! The air fares were complex and, with transfers, hotels and sightseeing in multiple destinations, it could be quite challenging, especially with my co-ordination. I settled down and in general I was pretty good at it. I never really set the heather alight but was average with my sales and good with my airfares.

Soon after joining, I had bought a fairly modern semi-detached house in the Pollok area of Glasgow. This was a decent place and there was less crime than there was in Muirhouse in Edinburgh, but the house was part of a similar regeneration thing. This ended up being the only house I've bought that I made a loss on!

About a year after joining, I was offered a special travel-agent trip to Australia! Again, I will document this in a separate travel chapter.

It was soon after returning from this trip that I had made a moderate mistake for which I ended up on some sort of action plan. I wasn't in major trouble, but it started to make me think again that there was a good chance I might be dyslexic. I mentioned it to my departmental manager. I decided not to pursue this possibility and tried just to be as accurate as I could; I think sometimes the pressure of avoiding mistakes can actually cause mistakes to happen. I was a bit stressed and worried about my job. I was, however, well-liked and had a supportive boss, Danielle, at this time, who has since lived and worked in Melbourne, Australia for a number of years. She still works in travel. I was also given the chance to go on a six-centre African trip on a hotel train, which was the best holiday I've had to date! My mistakes were never too bad and I actually survived two redundancy processes.

I went to lots of supplier nights and entered lots of competitions. I won two notable prizes—eight nights in luxury hotels in Thailand with the Starwood group, staying in lovely places and brands like Sheraton, Westin and Le Meridien. Again, I will cover this trip in another chapter. I also won a stay at One Devonshire Gardens, which had one of the best restaurants in Glasgow—even the whole of Scotland. This is where I had my only taste of eel, which isn't a dish I will have again!

I also helped my company by being in charge of a new online support team, providing support through instant messenger rather than phone. I had amazing feedback from some of our biggest clients, to the extent that the business won a Scottish award based entirely on this service.

* * *

A week before I left the company, I had a few drinks after work. I wasn't drunk and, again, it's interesting to look back when considering my dyspraxia, which I didn't know I had then. There was a manhole with no warning signs round a ninety-degree bend in the pavement. There were dark-green plastic barriers scattered on the ground; it looked like they had fallen in the wind. They looked as though they were designed for surrounding a toddler's Wendy house, not a four-foot manhole! I actually tripped on the barrier and fell headfirst down the hole. Some of my work colleagues witnessed this, and it was a sore one. I had loads of cuts, bruises and grazing, but luckily had not broken any bones. I had chipped some of my teeth and burst my front lip. I was taken to the hospital by ambulance, which in itself was a surreal experience as the accident happened only a few minutes' drive from the hospital. I was somewhat dazed and confused, and on arrival at hospital I actually said to the paramedics, "Oh no, we've broken down!" They said, "Actually, we're at the hospital!"

I was kept in for two nights and, for the first night,

the nurse would wake me hourly, take my blood pressure and ask me where I was. Partly due to my dyspraxia and dyslexia, I couldn't remember the name of the hospital—it was the Western or Southern, but I accidentally got it wrong every time—and who the prime minister was. Despite my injuries, I had not lost my sense of humour. I think I recalled all the prime ministers from Ted Heath onwards!

My clothes were totally bloodstained and I broke my specs. To this day, I have a numb top lip, and I'm told I will never get the feeling back due to nerve damage. I attempted to sue the City of Glasgow Council and persuaded four "no win no fee" solicitors to take me on, but the council just said they were not accepting my claim and every solicitor simply backed down. I was not brave or wealthy enough to go down the fee-paying option and feel very angry about the council refusing any sort of compensation. I never gave up, even after the four solicitors, and went on to involve my MP and MSP. I then had to draw a line under it!

* * *

My parting with this company was certainly not a bad one, and it remains my favourite place I've worked in. However, one bad thing happened that I've never understood. I went for a team leader job. I don't recall if it was just two of us that applied or if only two of us got shortlisted, but my colleague beat me to it and the only feedback I got was "I did poorly". This outcome was on the day I was leaving on a business-class Emirates flight to Thailand, so it wasn't the best news for my holiday. I pushed for feedback but never got it, and rather than give me any feedback, they offered me the new online support position without any process. However, I don't agree that I did poorly!

I'm not exactly sure what my motivation was but, after about three years, I felt I could run my own travel business and joined what is known as a homeworking company. I had looked at a few companies, but most would not take me forward with just a tour operator background apart from the one I joined. I had to present a business plan and made two trips to the company's HQ to convince them to take me on. This was good, as I had access to good systems and was able to give my customers the peace of mind of ATOL/ABTA protection. I probably used to be better at interviews than I am today!

For the first three months, I did quite well. My old colleagues, because they were trade only, had put a few friends and family referrals my way, and I was off to a good start. I had a number of marketing ideas, including trying to work with a Groupon-type deals company, but I never pulled this off. I had a number of meetings with a former Dumbarton footballer and, while he was keen to sort out the deal, I think his boss was a bit unsure. It was a deal with a free microchip-trackable luggage label and airport lounge package if a holiday of certain value was booked. I don't think this was going to make me or not.

Again, I won some things during this self-employment. I had another travel industry trip, this time to lovely Canada.

I also was runner-up in Travel Agent MasterChef. I just had to get myself to a lovely hotel west of London called Littlecote House. I was told there were hundreds of entries, but my dish of Thai green rabbit curry, all cooked from scratch, was a finalist.

It was an amazing experience. We had a tour of the splendid hotel, masterclasses from the executive chef and some of his team, and a photoshoot in the grounds, which ended up on the front cover of *Travel Weekly* magazine. There were three of us in the final. It was an interesting experience being in a professional kitchen. I was pleased with my dish, but it wasn't good enough to win. I was more than happy with how I had done. After the judging we all tried each other's dishes, then the three of us all had dinner together with some champagne and wine, and had a laugh about feeling that the hotel may be haunted. I had a four-poster bed in my room; it was lovely. I had breakfast with one of the other finalists the next day, then got the train back to Glasgow.

Soon after this experience, the business was really not working out. I had struggled with marketing and my self-employment and was relying heavily on referrals. I didn't want to close, but I had to take a serious look at my lack of regular and consistent income. I decided to go part-time with the travel business and look for a full-time job.

I didn't have to look hard as another large energy company was looking for folk. I was referred by a friend, and I actually wasn't shortlisted for interview, which is interesting in itself. I never really ask for help with applications, but I had started to consider my capabilities when filling out covering letters, CVs and application forms—was I doing something wrong? I never really got any meaningful feedback, but my friend who referred me went back to them, telling them that when he had worked with me, I'd been his favourite boss and surely they would interview me for an entry-level customer service role!

Thanks to Callum, they did interview me, and

when I get to an interview stage I usually do pretty well. I sailed through the rest of the process. I loved the training, which I excelled at, and my industry experience was useful.

On reflection, perhaps I wasn't any good at putting applications together, but I was interviewed for some community liaison officer position at the company in an attempt to get promoted and again the interview seemed to go ok. Bizarrely, to this day, I'm still waiting to hear if I got this job!? Clearly not, but that's just rude, isn't it? Sounds like something genuinely went wrong with the outcome letter—I did chase for it twice, then gave up. This did give a bad impression.

I had some really nice colleagues here. I'm still in touch with a few of them—Laura, Sara, whom I used to give a lift to work, and my good Irish friend, David, who now stays in Mull. I caught up with David and his wife, Maureen, recently, which was great. It was at this job that I decided my travel bug meant I wanted to get back in the industry, but I didn't want to risk giving up the main job. I never had the confidence to do only travel.

* * *

I had also taken in a lodger, Paul, who was a really nice fellow but sooooo clumsy—funnily enough, with my dyspraxia, my walking is quite clumsy but I don't really drop things and leave things on. Paul did stuff as serious as leaving the gas running on the cooker unlit and leaving the front door unlocked with his keys in the lock and borrowing money I had left for my cleaner.

I haven't really mentioned my cleaners, but over the years I've been blessed with amazing cleaners, many of whom are good friends to this day, so thank you to Debbie, Pauline, Jia, Karen, Michelle, Katie, the two Sarahs, Enid, Zara and Laura-Anne. I am scared of the iron, which I think is down to my dyspraxia, and I struggle to change the bed, given my problems with coordination. These ladies have been amazing, and I'm sure I will stay friends with many of them.

I applied for a home-based, salaried cruise sales company, just when I was aware that my current self-employment homeworking role had almost dried up. I had been threatened that they would close my business down due to consistent lack of sales. I was actually interviewed by the managing director of the cruise company. It was a tough process, and my roleplay was borderline. He said he would take a chance on me and took me to the next stage, which was to submit a travel blog. He really liked this, and yes, I had nailed this job.

I took my energy call centre job to part-time. They were quite good about this. This meant I would have about a fifty-hour week, which I managed fine.

During this time, I had sold my Glasgow house and decided to rent in Peebles. I regret only looking to rent in Peebles, and I made a loss on my Glasgow property.

One good thing about this job was that there was a golden welcome. I think it was £1500, but it was repayable if you didn't last three months. Out of my training group, only one person was still there last time I looked. I lasted about five months, which was longer than most of them and long enough to still keep the golden welcome. I had met all my staggered targets, but they seemed to feel I didn't quite have the knowledge, and they wanted me to exceed targets, not just meet them.

I was just back from a luxury cruise with my mum when I logged onto my company systems as the annual conference (held on a cruise ship) was only a few days away and I was really looking forward to it, a mini cruise to Bruges. I found out I was about to be fired as my name was taken off the list for this. My firing was unjust and not well handled.

I panicked a bit and did something stupid. I got caught too! I sent myself an email from my company laptop to my personal email address with some of my customer details. Part of the motivation for this was that they had asked constantly about what customer databases we had coming into the job, so clearly they were totally happy for us to bring our customers over, but were a bit hypocritical at the other end. I talked them into taking no further action against me. I therefore had to take the lessons learned and move on. While I was entitled to the data at my home as an employee, I wasn't at the point of leaving. With GDPR regulations, I would have been in big bother if this incident had happened more recently.

While I was glad I hadn't quit my now part-time energy job, I needed to have at least one full-time job. The energy company had twice adjusted my shift, and I decided Peebles to Cumbernauld was too much of a commute, especially part-time. Within about a week, I had managed to secure myself a full-time job for a small Borders-based energy company. This was ideal for me.

They were very nice during the process and delighted with how I did. Call centres do seem easier to get into in the Borders. This was a lovely place with nice people but was quite tight for space and calls were tough. We were multi-skilled, dealing with all energy enquiries.

I was rated highly and, after only two months, I was offered a promotion to complaints advisor. I was flattered by this but decided it was too soon into my time with the company, and I was also quite far into the extensive recruitment process for a banking job dealing with VIP customers. This was about a ten-step recruitment process, but things seemed to be going very well with it. Out of fairness to my employer, I wouldn't want to accept a promotion and then just leave.

Having worked about fifteen years in energy, I felt like a total industry change was due. I had a final interview, and then was called back for a personality/how-motivated-are-you type interview. Never had anything like this before, but again, I was really positive and ambitious and demonstrated I really wanted the job and got through. In addition to the CV, covering letter and application form there were about six online tasks and then the first interview, a roleplay, the second interview, then the motivational thing!

I got the job and there were about sixteen weeks of training! The trainers were great; they made the training such fun. There were only four of us in the training group, all nice people. It was interesting and intensive. I was dealing with normal transactional enquiries but also international payments, personal loans, credit card and overdraft applications.

We got famous people calling, which could actually be very daunting. During my training, where the time would be split between a few weeks in the classroom, then a few weeks in the academy taking calls in a heavily supported environment, I made a mistake during the customer identification process. These were considered to be among the more serious mistakes to make, and I then had to pass a few roleplays to get signed off. I failed the roleplays a few times.

I actually started to cry in the workplace and said that I thought I was dyslexic. I actually never wanted to have this conversation, as I felt that I didn't want to know, and I'd already got through twenty years in the workplace.

I felt trapped, and while the folk there were good about my thoughts, essentially, I had three options to choose from: 1. Do the assessment they had offered, and a workplace psychologist would come for an extensive meeting and reach a conclusion. 2. Do nothing and face the consequences of not getting through the roleplays and call assessments. There would be a high likelihood of me being managed out of the business. 3. Leave and move on or go back to something more familiar.

This was a traumatic time for me, a difficult decision. I had enjoyed the training a lot. The issues I had were following a script and being able to talk to the customer and choose the right options on the computer. It was like a flow chart: if they say this, click there, and so on.

I was feeling really low and also had flatmate issues, together with issues with my choice of flat. I'd made the choice of a flat in Peebles, right in the town centre, but it was near a rough pub. I will actually talk more about this incident in my political chapter, as I feel that story is relevant there.

My car got totally trashed in the carpark, and my flatmate also got his motorbike trashed. There were another two cars vandalised. This incident made me feel I had to move away from the pub area. I think my dyspraxia meant that noise could really affect my ability to relax and sleep more than most people.

Anyway, I decided that I would go through with

this psychological assessment. I had an extensive meeting at work, some paperwork was documented and the arrangements were made quickly. The assessment was to be about four hours long with a short break, and it was endless pages of exercises, some from a workbook and some involving motor skills and forming sorts of puzzles. At the start, the psychologist said he would write to me with the outcome. Despite thinking I'd done ok, it turned out my results were so strong that he actually told me the result was definite strong dyspraxia.

Prior to the report arriving back, me and my mum went through the symptoms of dyspraxia. In brief: a developmental disorder of the brain in childhood causing difficulty in activities requiring coordination and movement. The information I found went on to mention difficulties such as inability to ride a bike, clumsiness in walking and inability to do household chores, difficulty in concentration, nervousness in crowds and social awkwardness.

The report arrived after about a week, and it showed me to be highly dyspraxic and quite dyslexic. I had further discussions around support at work and the training team were great. This was an especially traumatic period for me and, at my stage in life, I didn't want to go through all this. I had mixed feelings, but to my credit, I was not off sick at all during this time. I pulled my socks up and decided I would work extra hard now I knew why I would sometimes struggle with things.

I was held back in a floor-walked environment for about an extra three months. While it was good to get the extra support, it also felt at the time like I was stupid, even though I couldn't help having the conditions.

When I did make it through the training stage,

I found the team environment really difficult. There was another guy in my team who was also dyspraxic. He never appeared to like me at all, and I think there was essentially an "I want to be the only dyspraxic person" attitude. While still in training, I was allowed to listen in to calls from my soon-to-be team members, and I never liked listening in with him. I empathised with him, but he was not at all interested in giving any assurance to me about coping with the condition.

I was only allowed into the team when my stats were around the expected figures, with a ten-percent adjustment made for my condition.

There was also a lady who came in from a government scheme called "access to work". I was given a grant to get counselling sessions, which I believe is normal for people being given news like this. These sessions were ok— quite useful in fact—and were for memory techniques and a general chat about my condition.

I asked the lady who came in if I had to mention having dyspraxia to future employers. She said no, and surprisingly said she thought employers would be less likely to employ someone dyslexic or dyspraxic, but if I struggled I might need to go through all the motions again. There used to be guaranteed interviews through a two-tick disability-friendly employer scheme. There is also something similar being set up that will help people in the near future.

The training people, especially the manager, Sam and deputy, Jim, were helpful and supportive. After I had maintained my targets and made it to my proper team with a stabilised performance for a few months, I was actually nominated for "new start of year" at the annual awards ceremony. This was a surprise and a real honour. I didn't win, but it was nice to be recognised. They could tell how difficult I had found things and how I'd made the effort to get through everything. I would say if you think you may be dyslexic or dyspraxic and you are under fifty and you're finding things even slightly tricky, it's usually best to get this recognised. I think that's a real reflection for me.

I had a good few months, but then things changed drastically. It was mainly my team's deputy that did the call assessment, and usually it was my manager who would give feedback, and these were some of the most negative things I've ever heard from any employer. I had really high scores from customer surveys, and I was generally passing the compliance side. I never had any major fails, having had the extra time in the training environment, but the soft skills feedback was so negative and de-motivational that I challenged it.

The bad stuff here was that the company had changed from a quarterly to annual bonus and that for challenging the feedback, which I did in a constructive way, my manager told me I was sitting on a zero multiplier for my bonus. This meant that any bonus would be multiplied by £0, so I would be getting nothing!

How could I be performing well, having gone through all I had, and then be told that—because of my alleged attitude—my bonus would be put to £0?

The deputy never liked me, even before I joined the team, and she went for me quite soon after joining. In fact, at a team meeting that I was invited to in order to get to know my new colleagues, one of the team invited me to a team night out, and then the deputy said it would be too much hassle and uninvited me! Quite an embarrassment, and not a good introduction to the new team! I got the feeling of dislike from her at this meeting, and it remained until I left. I was nice and polite to her despite everything she did, but she was constantly rude and unapproachable.

Another thing happened—quite a significant thing. A well-known TV presenter had called up, and I had serviced his call so well that he was totally delighted and wrote to his bank manager. I got feedback from the call centre manager, who read out the letter and gave me a pat on the back in praise, but again, my direct managers refused to recognise me for this.

I was missing the travel industry and I managed to persuade two travel companies to let me give homeworking another bash as a sideline, as I was not confident that I was making enough money full-time. I was brutally honest in saying marketing had let me down last time I tried this. Both said they appreciated my honesty. Having talked to me in detail, they both felt I was workable and, therefore, I had a choice to make. I was familiar with both options and there was not a lot to choose from; the decision was probably based on a residential training course in Blackpool that one was offering! I also felt that Peebles lacked a travel agent and, if successful, I had big ideas about enhancing the business into having a high-street presence.

The travel company gave me basic training. You had to already be fairly competent with industry knowledge to join, so it was more systems training. I managed with their help to get good local publicity with newspaper articles talking about my past round-the-world travels and cruise/travel background.

Unfortunately, it didn't lead to much in Peebles

and, despite a little help, I never managed to pull this off. I even had a launch event planned with Fred Olsen Cruises' backing. They were going to do a presentation about cruising from Scotland, but I only had a few people booked into this, so I decided to cancel it as it would not have been fair, especially as the Fred Olsen rep was based in Northern Ireland. After only three months, the travel company wanted to pull the plug, but I had just committed to an advert in a local directory that was about to be published. I persuaded them to give me another three weeks to see if we could produce any fruit, but this sadly was a complete disaster. I don't know why I was unable to pull this off, but this latest experience all but made me decide that self-employment is not for me.

* * *

I was feeling quite low at the main job, partly due to the sideline not working but also because I was still coming to terms with my dyspraxia and because I knew I was doing a good job and the subjective "attitude ratings" were just unfair. If I'd stayed and had not managed to move the rating out of "unacceptable", I would have considered raising a grievance.

I also had some additional health issues; I had a lump in my tummy and my doctor was concerned about it. I endured a number of checks and tests over a couple of months. The thing was that I had been offered a job with my former employer, back in the energy industry; however, I would be on unpaid absence if sick until through my probationary period, but I would have been paid if off sick at the bank.

I was honest with my manager, saying I was

likely now to be leaving but it was subject to getting through the medical checks. I ended up getting an ultra-scan and, to my great relief, it was a harmless lump.

Then I had the relief of leaving the bank. It was a stressful job dealing with high-value transactions, and I do accept the compliance and regulation aspects. I think this environment was too tough for me, and I was constantly under pressure and stress because of the number of calls monitored and the tough way they do—or certainly did—their feedback. I think this is the only employer I've ever had that would consider my "behaviour" enough of an issue to prevent me from earning a penny of annual bonus! Most other employers have actually given me extra bonus based on attitude or behaviour!

However, my exit here was quite dignified and tied in with a team Christmas night out taking place just after I had left. I was still invited to that, although I'm sure the deputy would have stopped me coming along if she could have! My advice is to always retain your grace and composure. The fact you don't give them a reaction shows strength of character.

It was strange to go back to a former employer, especially one that I had arguably had my best career at. My return was authorised at general manager level, and I don't believe there were any favours as I completed the application process. Billy from recruitment, however, was really patient with me, delaying the start date until I had the all-clear after the health scare.

The start date came around. I had slight nerves and was also quite excited, looking forward to catching up with old colleagues and all that. I was to work a four-day week on an 11:30-22:00 shift, or something close to that. I caught up with about twenty or thirty old colleagues on my first day and slightly fewer each subsequent day for a good month or so. Even two or three months in, I was bumping into people that I hadn't seen in about ten years.

On my application, I had been totally honest and declared myself as disabled, mentioning specifically my dyspraxia and dyslexia. I stated that I felt with my background—previously making it to departmental manager level—and with my other industry and general call centre experience, I didn't see my disabilities causing too much of an issue.

The training was more fun than anything, no fault of the trainers, but really it was a bit content-sparse and I would say that it was probably about fifty-to-sixty percent larking around. On reflection, with how my training group did, we really were set up to fail, but we did have great fun.

We played a lot of games and did fun exercises, and a lot of this was to help with team working/ group skills. My background was really useful, and I sailed through all the tests. In fact, on one test only two of us passed and I think, at this stage, our trainer realised that she had to put more focus on training us for the technical knowledge required. Everyone eventually got through all the modules, as you were allowed two resits if you failed any test, and everyone just managed that.

It really never felt the same working back there. It was as if my previous nine-year period had not happened. I also got offered a place on the Channel 4 TV show *15-1*, but management refused to give me the time off, which again made me unhappy, but as I was still on probation, I had to just accept it! I found there to be many inconsistencies, which drove me to look at work from a new, more negative perspective than the last time I was there!

Eventually I got my targets reduced and, soon after this, I was made permanent. It was a hard journey, and there no longer seemed to be the great career opportunities of last time round. Initially, I never felt valued, and it was a pretty miserable time.

This prompted me to go in a different direction, which was to be a champion of the people. I did this by becoming a trade union representative.

I was feeling a bit down and, together with renting rather than owing my property, I felt stuck in a bit of a rut.

I was now trying to sort my finances, which were a bit grim. I thought long and hard about the solutions, and the only obvious one was to do a more substantial second job.

I then joined a horrible telecoms call centre in South Lanarkshire. It was a bit of a trek from Peebles; the commute was tough in the winter. It wasn't too bad to start though. Training was ok, although after the first three weeks the main trainer left and, after that, we had about four or five different trainers. We were often forgotten about, and there were some days that we couldn't even get headsets and literally did nothing!

I think we all started part-time. There were fifteen of us to start with. (This was my special edition of *15-1*!) I don't think any of us were fired, but the calls were horrible and there was almost no structure. I think about three of the group left before the training finished. Someone just walked out a few days after training with loads of tears.

There were two dramatic leavers with big letters to the bosses about how bad things were.

There was total hot-desking almost everywhere. It was one of these jobs where you almost never existed. People were off all the time; I was off a fair few times, and sometimes I was brutally honest in saying I was too tired to come to work! Pay was minimum wage. It was the ugliest, most horrible call centre I've ever been in. The supervisors were mainly unhelpful. One of them even said to me he had no interest in helping me; he refused even though he was the duty supervisor and was responsible for helping people who were stuck!

About six months in, it was just me and Maryiam left. She changed her shift to evenings to accommodate her college course, so I would only ever catch up with her via Facebook. She was last person standing, so won our edition of *15-1*! I did get on it after all!

I was pretty average and, what with quite poor training and support, it was sometimes difficult. I was surprised that with my dyspraxia and dyslexia I was actually able to resolve a lot of the technical issues. Just because of the poor structure, sending an engineer was always an easy cop-out, especially given how difficult asking for help was. This was my second job, and early into the new year I was hoping to find an exit strategy.

I really liked the team; we looked out for each other. I'm still Facebook friends with a lot of the team and actually went to my friend Ashley's 30th birthday. There were meant to be some of the others there; nobody else made it, but that was ok. It was nice to catch up with her, although I'm not sure if I will meet up with any of the old team again.

I was lucky to have noticed much the same role

advertised (again through an outsourcing company) in the Borders. I sailed through the interview, although I got the feeling that almost everyone would pass the interview! The recruiter, Samantha, was so nice though, and I felt really valued.

I was so pleased to be able to leave the Lanarkshire job. I went in for my shift and said I would be starting a new job in a week's time. My manager asked if I wanted to do the week's notice or just leave! I said up to her, I could do the week if she wanted; she said totally my shout, so I did that day's shift, then just left! Because all my friends had already left, and Maryiam was on a totally different shift, nobody said bye at the end of my last shift! It had been only six months, but it's sad in some ways that you can be so invisible.

* * *

I had a week before starting the new part-time job. I mentioned to my boss at the main job about the new job and the impact of my training. I had now moved to a tougher shift in terms of the hours (18:00-02:00), although it was a better shift in terms of employee satisfaction.

I was pleased to join John's team. I've known him for around twenty years. I was already good friends with Graeme and I knew a lot of the rest of the team, such as Lisa and Stephen. This immediately helped me relax and feel more secure.

My boss was also sort of ok with the full-time training, knowing it was only going to be for two weeks. This meant almost an eighty-hour working week! It meant hardly any sleep but, somehow, I just about got through this. Day two in training at the new job, I was ten minutes late (and they were meant to have a three-strikes-and-you're-out policy). The trainer said how much he hated lateness! I pulled him aside later that day explaining my predicament and said I hoped this would just be a one-off but I couldn't promise. He was appreciative that I had told him about my circumstances and assured me he would be a bit more flexible with me, which was decent of him, especially as it was my issue and not his or the company's.

I was lucky to have had some skills/knowledge from the other telecoms job and muddled through the training half-asleep but felt I still had a fairly good understanding. The trainers were good, fun people. There was a good balance of having a laugh and serious job stuff. We then went into a floor-walked environment. There wasn't really the spirit within the training group of new starts that there was at the Lanarkshire job. There were four people meant to be doing the same shift as me, but a few weeks into the job two of them had left, leaving just me and Sarah. She was in a different team, but at weekends we would sit next to each other to help each other out.

It was a bit better than Lanarkshire. Supervisors did try to help the staff more, and there was more acceptance for manager call-backs, but it was still not a great place to work. I had an incident of intimidation from one of the managers. I could have taken it further and did raise an informal complaint. The manager kept repeating, "You've been in wrap for five minutes." Each time he said it louder and louder, pointing at me. Never understood if he was being serious in his conduct or if it was some practical joke?! I never got an apology, but I said wouldn't turn it into a grievance as long as didn't happen again.

I've been working there about a year and a half now and had to remind my boss that it had been almost a year since I last had any feedback whatsoever. This has since been resolved since Danni took over the team. He is quite like-minded and is a 'people ahead of process' person, and this has probably kept me there as the extra money is handy, although no longer needed. Until Danni took over, I felt invisible and, on some shifts, I didn't have any interaction with any other staff, just came in, took calls and went home; no development, no atmosphere, just another horrible, gloomy call centre. This second job does however still serve its purpose financially. I will talk about why I'm still here in my chapter about the future, as I do have good reasons why I've never left.

* * *

I also managed to pick up sort of a third job, with a travel representation company! It's like doing ad-hoc PR on behalf of some travel tour operators and cruise companies and doing high street travel agency visits. I've had about seven assignments in roughly a three-year period, and this is totally fine; it keeps my feet in travel as I really miss being full-time in the travel industry. My favourite assignments were mystery shopping; great fun!

Overall, the second-job situation has really helped my financial situation out greatly and helped me keep on traveling, which is an area I will never stop making the most of.

When the landlord of my Edinburgh Road rental sold the house to another landlord, I quickly sensed that she was going to be hard work. Initially, this house was a good move. The previous landlord was happy to just take my money each month, but the new owner was one of these stifling people who was too much as a landlord. She was always in the garden, at least once or twice a week. I had no privacy. She was getting fairly substantial maintenance work done to the house that most people would only do to a vacant property. Fair enough, to an extent, that she was a little reluctant to buy the house with a sitting tenant. All things said, I let the previous tenancy end early, knowing the new landlord was going to raise the rent quite significantly. Essentially my cooperation meant I let both landlords get away with not giving me notice of the changes! This also helped her avoid new legislation in buy-to-let stamp duty by days, saving her a very substantial four-figure sum, but she still put the rent up considerably!

I ended up hating the situation. I also had issues with flatmates and was regretting being off the property ladder. My debts were more manageable, but I didn't have a deposit saved to go back to owning my own home. I asked my mum for help and, with her kindness, she agreed, and I was able to get back on the property ladder. I offered my flatmate the chance to move with me but secretly hoped he wouldn't do so. I offered him the room at a fair price, and he said he would only take it for a cheaper price, so I said, "Not negotiating, but all the best...". I never gave him the chance to change his mind or negotiate it, and while this meant finding a new lodger, I was quite pleased. I'd got on with most of my past lodgers, but he seemed to wind me up. I had selflessly given him the biggest bedroom and done my best to be accommodating with him, having his kids at weekends, etc., but his habits of leaving lights and the shower thermostat on were really annoying, especially with huge energy bills of over £250 a month! There were other issues, but in the main I felt a lack of respect toward me, although again, life's too short, and I seem to have resolved many of our differences. I think this was a lesson that it's better to have a stranger than a friend as a lodger.

I can't thank my mum enough. She had helped me get my new place and initially it felt good. It had a trendy kitchen, a rainforest shower and a Jacuzzi bath! It was priced well under the survey value as it was a builder's trade-in. However, it was a flat-roofed property and, soon after moving in, I had a leaky roof and a bit of damp in a few of the rooms. I had an insurance policy with home emergency cover and they called out the next day and put in some roof filler, but their report indicated the roof was in bad order. A few months later, with torrential rain, the water came in again, but this time much worse. I needed a claims assessor, and I got some quotes. I spent a few thousand pounds on quite a lot of roof work.

It wasn't too bad, as I had actually prudently bought this place with a view of selling within about a year, knowing I had bought well under market value. I did sell within the year. Not for an amazing price, but I had made £6,000, even after the roof repairs, and therefore I was able to pay my mum back the rest of the money she had lent me to pay for my flat's deposit. I had been paying her a monthly amount, but it was a good feeling to pay the rest off and, again, I was so grateful for my mum's help. I took her and her partner, Jim, for a two-night stay at one of my favourite Scottish hotels, New Lanark Mill, as a thank you. Had a brilliant time there, as ever. Will cover trips like this in more detail in my chapter about my travels.

I've side-tracked a bit, and you can see how busy I have been—possibly why I've been writing this for three years and I'm only on chapter five! Although, as you will have read, this is by far the longest chapter in the book.

Back to my main job, and I do like my teammates. We've had some good nights out, and there's always good banter in the team to get us through till 2 a.m. Post my probation period, it's a good place to work, but just frustrating that I can't seem to make the same progress I made last time I worked here. I am not sure exactly why. I may need to get more opinions on my CV and covering letter. Perhaps I'm not in the modern world and need to understand more about what employers are looking for these days?

I don't have any intention to leave the business, as pensions and salary are pretty decent. Scary thing is I am over halfway through my working life. I've always had a fear of getting older and worry about death and what happens when you die. I would describe myself as a non-practicing Christian—you will have read more on this in my college chapter.

So that's it for my employment and self-employment. I'm sure there will be some stuff to add on. If there is a second edition of this book, I will advise what has happened since 2018!

CHAPTER 6

Relationships

I've not talked a lot about girlfriends during my writing. In truth, that's because there's not much to tell here, but I'm sure it's not a coincidence that I had a bit more luck finding a girlfriend during the times I was on a better shift. Generally, I met everyone through online dating.

My first proper partner was Karen, a nursery nurse from Glasgow. She was really nice, softly spoken, very caring and quite trendy as well. I met her through online dating and over the next four months or so, we ended up having about eight or nine dates. We first met at Boozy Rouge, a restaurant I quite liked in Glasgow, and our other dates tended to be eating out again or going to the cinema. I also cooked her a meal at my flat once. She let me down quite gently, advising me that she was soon going to move to Dubai to become a DJ. She was also a hideous driver, always calling or texting me while driving. She also had a habit of parking in spaces smaller than her car! Never seen such a bad driver—she told me about several crashes she'd been in. I don't think we were very compatible, but I am so glad to have dated her as she helped no end with my self-confidence.

My next partner was Debbie. We were together for about nine months. We would mainly do turnabout at each other's place; she was from Stirling which wasn't too far. She also worked in a call centre but for a bank. We had a lot in common, and she was probably even softer spoken than Karen. She was quite forward with me, and I was excited—I loved going to her flat.

Things seemed to be going really well until the night of my thirtieth birthday celebration. I think she had planned on leaving me but was like a drama queen! I had told her that she was to come round to my Edinburgh flat for 3 p.m. on the afternoon of my birthday to then head into town. I left further messages for her when she didn't arrive, but by about half four we had to go—in fact, my family had actually arranged a stretch limo for me. She called me when I was in the restaurant, telling me she wasn't comfortable about arriving there on her own and told me where to go!

Then I dated Lucy, who was a second child from China and told me sad stories about life in China being difficult, especially with the one-child policy. I lived very near Lucy, about a fifteen-minute walk away, which was handy.

Our first date was a pretty awful meal in Café Rouge, but she suggested going to a nice bar afterwards and we agreed to have another date. Things went well and, after a number of dates, we agreed to a weekend in Dumbarton!

She would sometimes go to the Dumbarton games with me. When I wanted to take her round Loch Lomond, she was a bit odd. She said she was unwell and wanted to go back to Edinburgh, but the moment we got back in the car, she said she was better but still wanted to go back home.

As well as dining out, we would often dine in, go to the cinema, Fringe shows etc. We also went to the Lake District to a hotel I liked, but shortly after booking, she produced the bombshell that suddenly her flatmate and best friend, Ellen, wanted to come as well—two's-company, three's-a-crowd type stuff!

The moment we checked in, Ellen declared she only had two days off work and couldn't manage the three-night stay, so we needed to cancel the last night. I told Ellen I would drop her off at the train station after the first two nights! She wasn't happy with this, but unfortunately managed to get the third night off.

It was my birthday while we were away. I had lovely chats with Lucy, and she got upset and declared her real name was actually Haifei and thought I would be angry with her. I understood the Asian culture of often having a Western name as well as her given name. She seemed relieved; overall the weekend had gone ok but having her housemate there was a bit weird.

Things were fine during the months following this. She had often met my friends, who all liked her, and I loved socialising with friends and her. She refused to meet my family though—seemed to be a ritual thing that our relationship had to be really advanced before she'd do that.

Our one-year anniversary approached, and I booked a romantic meal at the MacDonald Holyrood (not the burger place, but a really nice hotel restaurant). We started to have a nice meal, but towards the end, she declared that she had been seeing someone else for some time and essentially made out that we had always been just good friends and nothing more. I disputed this and didn't take it at all well, but kept my cool and agreed to stay in touch as friends. We met up two or three times after that and got on well, but overall, I was sad and never really got over her. She came through to Dumbarton to see me, and I met her in Edinburgh a couple of times after we split. Prior to our split, I also helped teach her to drive.

* * *

I bounced back from Lucy quite quickly. In fact, within weeks of moving to Dumbarton, my upstairs neighbour Julie called round to my flat in tears. Her boyfriend was in jail, and she thought she'd heard people trying to break into her flat and was scared. I let her in, gave her some coffee, then wine, and comforted her. I didn't hear anyone, but a few months after this I was burgled myself.

We became very good friends and started to develop a fantastic relationship. We were both nervy living in Westcliff, Dumbarton, as it was rougher than I appreciated, but Julie was affectionate, caring and romantic.

She would call round my flat most nights for a glass of wine and to watch a film or TV. She was the most romantic lover I've had, and when her partner was released from jail, she continued to spend loads of time with me. He never appeared to mind, and I think they were drifting apart in any case.

There was an occasion that really finished our relationship where, when I went to the toilet and came back, about £50 had vanished. Unfortunately, while this was the only incident I ever had with her, I struggled to trust her after this. After this happened, things were not the same and I never really spent much time with her again.

When she fully split with her partner soon after

this, they gave up the flat. Julie was then staying with a friend a few miles away in Bonhill. She called and texted me loads of time one night. Gauging her despair, I got back to her. She said her friend had to give up her flat, and she literally had nowhere to stay. She asked to stay over at mine. I reluctantly agreed but I found it hard to trust her—I actually hid my cards and cash!

I was moving house the next day and it was a bit of an inconvenience, but I also felt for her. If she had asked to borrow or even just asked if I would let her have the money without repaying. I would have said yes; I don't hold a grudge though. We had a lovely night together. Shared a lovely meal, nice wine, and it was lovely sharing the bed! Given our past relationship being so sweet, neither of us wanted to be in different beds! She also pressed me about moving in with me permanently. It was hard for me, my heart wanted to say yes but my head was saying no. We shed a few tears that night and the next morning.

She wanted me to drive her all the way to a friend's house in Pitlochry, but I reminded her how hectic my day was going to be with the house move.

I dropped her at the train station, leaving her with enough money to get to Pitlochry and get a coffee and a sandwich. We exchanged a few texts after this, and then we seemed to lose contact. I think when I changed phones, not all my contacts had saved. I miss Julie terribly; she's the only person whom I've ended a relationship with, the rest ended things with me. You could say we had an affair, but from my explanation, you may appreciate the complexities of our relationship!

* * *

My last partner was in around 2008. Interestingly, all my partners were in succession; there was at most only a few months' gap between partners— not long at all over a few years. Was this down to me being more confident then? Slimmer? Better looking? Luckier? I've not really been trying for the last while as my focus has been more on just getting by and, due to multiple jobs, I don't really have much time.

This has now changed and I'm having some luck with online dating. It's all feeling a bit weird and I'm making a real effort; I regret not doing more the last ten years or so. I think I had been stressed/depressed, had lost a fair bit of self-esteem and had some challenging times in the workplace, which had made it difficult for me to feel comfortable enough with relationships. I think with my dyspraxia, communication is never easy. If something becomes too complex, I can give up. I essentially gave up for around ten years, and now, in my forties, I feel sad about this lost time. I had been treading water a bit with stuff like debt, and life and work had become more challenging in many respects!

CHAPTER 7

Holidays

Travel is a big part of my life. It is one of the main things I enjoy in my spare time, so I have written quite a lot about all my holidays. This chapter covers my main holidays while my travel industry trips are in another. Another is on my round-the-world trip, where I wrote a travel diary, and there's another on the cruises I've done!

I liked our family holidays, they were always exciting. My memories go back to when I was only three years old. Back when my sister and I were very young, our family holidays were generally to Carradale or Arran. We would often holiday with friends of the family, the Kennedys; their daughters were of similar age to us and we would all get on well together—I could somehow cope with being the only boy!

* * *

Carradale, Scotland

We would often stay at the same boarding house in Carradale and have bed, breakfast and dinner. It was a very traditional set-up with quite a strict landlord; we kids would always need to be on our best behaviour.

The holidays to Carradale were very pleasant. Nice walks, playing with a kids' fishing net in rockpools, swimming in the sea and enjoying the beach. Generally, I only recall good weather back then, in the late 1970s to early 1980s.

Near Carradale is a town called Campbeltown, which was pretty rundown. I didn't enjoy visiting Campbeltown, as my feet were like magnets when we were there, and I ALWAYS used to stand on dogs' dirt. Again, like in primary school, not deliberate—I just couldn't help myself. Was this a dyspraxia-related issue? I would guess it was. Quite often it would be the almost-mythical white dogs' dirt! It really did exist—my friend Graeme believed it was bone marrow that caused the poo to be white?! A quick Google search has confirmed this to be accurate!

Arran, Scotland

Arran was very similar. These places were a long drive away, but we had good fun. We enjoyed scenic drives, and even at a young age, it made me appreciate how nice places in Scotland are.

Early memories I have of Arran are going to

the aptly named Blackwaterfoot swimming pool. Even as a three- or four-year-old, I had hygiene standards, and that minging pool was not meeting them. I had a total screaming fit—and I really can remember this far back in the 1970s!

I remember playing pitch-and-putt a few years later and being just about as bad back then as I am now! I'm ok at a putting green or crazy golf, but not on a pitch-and-putt or full golf course. However, I would like to take up the game at some point!

St Andrews, Scotland

I also recall a few trips to my gran's caravan in the lovely town of St Andrews. My sister and big cousin Graeme couldn't be bothered with me on one occasion, and there were big metal cage-like things—something to do with bin storage, probably—on the caravan site, and I was told to "be a lion". That meant me then sitting in the cage and actually roaring at everyone who walked past me—not sure how long they left me!

Visiting St Andrews was all about nice ice cream. There was every flavour under the sun, even back in the early 1980s, and lovely beaches. We also watched the golf Open a few years later, which was a nice memory.

* * *

As me and Carole grew older, the next few holidays were to English cities.

York, England

I loved our trip to York in the early 1980s. We had seen the Jorvik Viking Museum on the kids' TV programme *Blue Peter* and were excited to go there and go back in time on the time car feature. The Castle Museum was great. I also loved the Rail Riders miniature railway—I had free or discounted entry to loads of these places due to my Rail Riders card (I remember the Rail Riders jersey Mum knitted me). The rail museum is also a great place; I've been back there three or four times since then.

We loved our hotel, which is still there—the Lady Ann Middleton Hotel. This was the first hotel we stayed at where we had a steam room, sauna and Jacuzzi. We felt quite grown-up when Mum and Dad let us use these.

London, England

Next break was another real adventure—a trip to London by train. I was so excited, as I was (or rather still am) obsessed with the London Underground, and I was finally getting to go on it.

We did all the usual things—Madame Tussaud's waxworks, the Transport Museum, Harrods famous department store, the mammoth toy store Hamleys. I can remember the excitement of choosing a toy, and I think my parents were impressed that I chose a sensible option of a lovely Pelham puppet, which I still have. I named him Claudio, after my Chilean friend.

I loved going on a classic 1960s London routemaster bus. I think the highlight of this trip was a visit to The London Palladium to see Michael Crawford (who made his name as the hapless Frank Spencer in the sitcom *Some Mothers Do Have 'Em*) in *Barnum*. He was amazing and did all the circus skills stunts.

The whole Barnum thing has come back round with the musical film *The Greatest Showman*. I recommend this film—a cracking and true story and, as a disabled person, there are some really interesting lessons on diversity and controversy.

Another London family trip, doing much the same activities and museums, involved a trip to *Singin' in the Rain* with well-known West End veteran performer Tommy Steele, who is still active at the time of writing, despite being in his eighties.

London and Paris

This trip was our first time abroad. It was an amazing trip. I was so excited to be going abroad. I think this was my first time on a plane, London-Paris-Edinburgh. When we arrived in Paris, it was manic. The taxi queue was crazy, and the drivers were reluctant to take four people, even though they all had three seats in the back and the front passenger seat.

I remember being excited and looking forward to trying snails—which I did! I was an experimental eater, even as a young kid. We did the Eiffel Tower—Dad even coped with his fear of heights—plus Notre Dame, the Champs-Elysees and the Louvre, to see the famous Mona Lisa. We loved the modern art gallery and the Pompidou centre. I loved our first meal in a nice restaurant, but our second meal—at a Greek place—was probably a bit too different for Carole and me at the time. Nowadays, though, I love Greek food. Even the fear of drinking tap water was alien to us—it was the first place we'd ever been where you shouldn't drink tap water. Was a great experience though.

Isle of Man, UK

Our next trip was a nostalgic one for Dad, as it took him back to a childhood holiday destination, and was a trip to the lovely Isle of Man. We stayed in

Port Erin, which was also where Dad stayed on his childhood trip. This was a great holiday. We met nice kids at the beach. I loved the vintage public transport network, which is practically unchanged to this day and involves a steam railway line between Port Erin and the capital, Douglas. There was an electric mountain railway line and horse-drawn trams in Douglas.

My sister won a talent contest—singing, I think—at our hotel. I can't recall if I entered this contest or just watched.

I remember us experiencing a minor earthquake when here. We also got the car ferry from Heysham near Morecambe.

I would like to go back there—would have also been nice to take my son had I been a father.

Amsterdam
Next up was a trip to Amsterdam. I have a feeling this was a last-minute trip and recall something about an airline or travel company going bust and this being some sort of replacement trip.

This was another amazing trip, again all about culture. Anne Frank's house, the Rijks Museum and Gallery, pedalo on the canals, canal boat trip. Dutch pancakes with ice cream and Nutella! I loved the friendliness of the city. I've since returned here loads of times.

France
My next trip was actually a first-year high school trip to Calais by bus. It was on this trip that I had a fling with a senior pupil. I was only in first year and I think she was in fifth year—quite an age gap! Her name was Wendy.

It was a brutal trip by bus and ferry, but an

adventure! This was towards the end of the bad period when I was having nightmares, and I think I was partly anxious about being away from home without my parents. I think the only other times I'd stayed away from my parents would have involved staying at my Aunt Betty's while Mum and Dad went to Bath and another time to Brussels in Belgium.

What was interesting was me winning the quiz prize; perhaps other folk couldn't be bothered, as I was not doing all that well with my French in the classroom. The prize was an error— a weird comic book that soon drew a crowd on the bus as it contained naked cartoon ladies! The French teacher who presented me with this embarrassingly tore all the nude pictures out, then gave it back to me!

London and France

Next up was a brutal sleeper train trip to London for me, Mum and Carole. It was like a never-ending nightmare, but not quite enough to put me off my love of trains! I recall some youths sleeping on the ceiling luggage racks, the seats were that uncomfortable. I also remember us arriving at our London hotel and being told it had been overbooked; we ended up being upgraded.

This was now our third trip to London, and as well as all the usual stuff, Mum got to choose the show! She chose her favourite singer, Cliff Richard, in *Time*. There were lots of special effects, and I think we all enjoyed it, especially Mum!

This was to be an epic trip to the Loire valley. We met Dad in Portsmouth, as he was taking the car through to France. I also remember being so tired on the ferry from Portsmouth that I fell asleep right away, and again, we were on recliner chairs.

For me, it felt like the ferry journey only lasted five minutes, but I'm sure it was a different story for the rest of the family!

We had a great trip but there was a lot of driving. Dad did well to manage all this. We stayed at a chalet-campsite-type place, and this was amazing. I remember the wonderful langoustines, whole in the shells. One of the hotels in Normandy served an amazing seafood pie, rich with lovely crab and other things.

I remember Carole trying to put her French high school skills into practice, and the barman was rolling about on the floor as she almost ordered twelve glasses of Coke instead of the required two! To be fair, the French words for two and twelve are very similar!

France
Next was another school trip. We stayed at a horrible hotel in Fontainebleau. I shared a room with Keith and Brian, and we only had a double and a single bed, so we took turns to use the single bed. I remember the walls being rotten and them punching the walls and denting them—I assure you I wasn't involved in this! They didn't face any consequences for it, though!

Other than the hotel, this was a decent trip with nice people. It was a coach trip again, and we went to Paris for at least one day. I met some nice people from school that I hadn't previously come across; this was a second-year trip. I was very lucky to get these trips.

Aviemore/Meigle, Scotland
Had some other trips without my family. Some were with the Sunday Group, which was a youth-club-

type thing set up by the local church. I recall going to Aviemore Youth Hostel and loving Aviemore. It was quite run-down back then but had a certain appeal.

Another trip was to Meigle in Perthshire. I think these were just short two-night stays, Friday and Saturday.

Yugoslavia

After the previous years' successful trips to France, Dad decided to go for something a bit different. He chose really well—we were off to Yugoslavia. We would have been in third year at high school.

Like most of our holidays back then, there was a brutal start with a seemingly never-ending drive to Luton. Dad contemplated us hoteling overnight but chose instead to drive through the night from Peebles!

With all our trips, we always had complicated UK journeys. We then had big delays at the airport! This was with an airline that somehow has survived, and I'm sure are a lot better now! I'm sure after our nightmare journey to Luton the plane was delayed a good three or four hours, or more. We were all knackered! Mum had bought me a shell suit to be more comfortable on the plane. I had done work experience at the local sports shop, and she took me there as a treat—was the height of fashion!

On arrival at Split we had to get a hydrofoil to the island of Brač. I remember it being a bumpy journey with rough seas.

We were all knackered on arrival, but after a great night's sleep, we were all delighted to wake up the next day in a lovely resort hotel. The facilities were decent, especially for a communist country. There was a lovely swimming pool, an open-air cinema with films in English, an amazing beach and the famous Zlatni Rat Beach. I loved swimming in the sea and going out on the pedalo boats with my sister. Great food. We met such nice people—I recall a young couple who liked me and my sister and took us to the cinema one night. Children were allowed alcohol from about the age of fourteen, and Mum and Dad allowed me and Carole to have a couple of drinks. The cinema was licensed, and the drinks were practically free! I was allowed a beer when watching the films, and after dinner I would sometimes have a mish-mash, which was half red wine and half orange juice. I think my favorite though was the homemade lemonade, which was freshly squeezed lemon juice, sugar and water, but so tasty!

I remember a nice day trip to Dubrovnik—such a stunning city—and although me and my sister were on the young side, we still appreciated how lovely it was!

We flew home on an ancient Russian aircraft. Several engineers boarded, which was not too reassuring, and then from our seat by the wing, we saw and could smell fuel! Twenty minutes into the flight, the captain advised we were being diverted due to technical problems and actually made an unscheduled emergency landing in Ljubljana. Loads of fire engines greeted us after landing. Mum and Dad were petrified, but I was enjoying the adventure! A few hours later, and we seemed to be ok to fly back to Luton. We made it back ok!

Overall, the trip to an unspoilt part of Eastern Europe had been such a success that we opted for a similar trip the following summer but to a different resort. We flew JAT (Yugoslavian Aerotransport) this time. I think had it not been for Adria Airways, we would have probably gone back to the same resort! Much the same trip—another great success!

West Highland Way, Scotland

Our next holiday was one of the best. Again, we were back to the lovely country we live in, and we were walking the West Highland Way. We did it in reverse, starting at the official end in Fort William and ending in Milngavie at our friends' house (Mum was born in Milngavie and wanted to "walk home"). This was a good way to do it, and we had a great time.

We took the train on the scenic route to Fort William, and then the walking holiday began. We all coped pretty well. The first day was near Ben Nevis, the biggest mountain in the UK. We stayed in nice places on this trip—a mix of quality bed-and-breakfast establishments and hotels. We were very lucky with the weather, can't recall any rain the entire week! We were walking ten to fifteen miles every day, but we were all relatively healthy. We always had a nice meal to look forward to in the hotel or B&B each night and a good breakfast at the start of each day.

Some places were memorable for being really bad, such as Bridge of Orchy. I know it has since changed hands, and I'm sure it's nice these days. When we were there and arrived for dinner, the grumpy waitress repeated, "Have you booked? Have you booked?" while we looked into the empty restaurant! We could hear the ping of the microwave oven going the whole time, and our food was not the freshly made offering we expected! A French couple were asked what wine they'd ordered about four or five times before it finally arrived. There was a used nappy in the bin in our family room. I sort of expected to see Basil Fawlty kicking about!

In contrast, the very remote Kingshouse was like a real oasis. It was amazing, like a private country mansion in the middle of nowhere, and we had a fantastic stay with amazing food!

We managed most of the walk ok. Some days were hard going in warm weather. Queen Elizabeth Forest Park and the stunning Loch Lomond stretch was particularly tough, with steep drops and my dad's fear of heights!

It was great to be welcomed back to Milngavie by the Kennedys, lifelong friends of my family, who hosted us that night. We had enjoyed a fantastic holiday and a great adventure.

Sicily, Italy

I've not really counted it as holiday, but I covered Borders Youth Theatre (BYT) and Scottish Youth Theatre (SYT) in my high school section. I'm mentioning it now because Carole hated our next trip as she missed what was probably the BYT production she most wanted to be in—a musical called *Thin Image* about an anorexic girl. Her then boyfriend, Ewan, was in the band, so she was likely to be missing him!

The holiday to Sicily was also sort of our last family trip. We stayed at a nice hotel with a reputation for quality water sports—things like sailing and windsurfing. I think this would have just about kept my sister a little enthused, but it was so windy the whole time that there was actually no sailing or windsurfing available!

Furthermore, Carole hated the food and got stung by a jellyfish! Also, the only other thing she wanted to do was to see the volcano Mount Etna, and Mum and Dad—for what reason I can't recall—decided against this!

I had a nice time. I remember showing off in the outdoor pool to two stunning local Italian ladies a year or two older than me. I was a slim lad back then, believe it or not!

We went on some long and dangerous walk, which included being by a fast road and dodging the oncoming cars! I remember seeing a snake on the same walk.

Carole also caught me reading her diary, which was a naughty thing to do! For some bizarre reason, through my radio/alarm clock back at home, I could hear family members' and neighbours' phone calls. Again, I got some telling offs for misusing this situation! Generally, I was not too badly behaved!

Australia

Carole had now finished high school, and I was entering sixth year. She had decided to take a gap year out to Australia, and we went to meet her at the home of friends of the family in Canberra and then took her with us to the Barrier Reef in Cairns. We left for this trip a few days before Christmas, and it was for around three weeks. The school cooperated, given the nature of the holiday— I was a sixth-year pupil in any case—allowing me the extended holiday.

It was really snowy when leaving for Edinburgh airport, but we gave ourselves plenty of time and were flying British Airways to Heathrow, connecting with Qantas to Australia via Bangkok. Mum had a bit of an issue at check-in, but at least our luggage was now checked in all the way to Sydney. There was huge excitement, especially from me and Mum as we had never flown long-haul before. Dad was used to flying to America and Asia on business, being a director of textile companies. In fact, he had recently flown out to New York with British Airways first class and Concorde! He had also recently flown to Singapore in Singapore Airlines business class, so he was used to flying in style. We obviously were in economy; in fact, it was probably dearer to fly to Australia back then than it is now. I'm sure it was about £1,000 each back then, although these were peak dates and it was the height of summer in Australia.

Back in 1991, technology wasn't the same as now, so there were communal TVs, possibly just a few of them for the whole of economy. There was no personal choice of films, although the films were fairly decent. I definitely remember watching the great film *Trading Places*. My mum is puzzled by my memory—I seemed to remember trivial things like what the carpet in the hotel looked like, but struggled to remember important things like the lines for the play I was in; but these are typical traits of people that have dyslexia or dyspraxia!

I also remember episodes of a 1950s America sitcom called *I Love Lucy* being played—not got a clue why?! Also, *Mr Bean* programmes.

I was allowed to have beer and the food was decent. I struggled to sleep, though. In fact, I've never been able to sleep well on flights, even ones with the posh seats!

It was a relief to stretch our legs in Bangkok for a few hours, then it was back on board the same plane heading for Sydney. It was definitely exciting to be going to Australia and flying halfway round the world. Before long, we had landed in Sydney and our friendly taxi driver kindly gave us a talk, like an overview of the city.

I can remember never being so tired. It was full-on not to waste any time with the thirty hours or so we had in this amazing city. I remember Dad telling me off for my mouth being open, but I think this was just down to me feeling like a zombie! I practically fell asleep as we were driving over the iconic Sydney Harbour Bridge—I just couldn't stay awake anymore! I have no recollection of even having dinner; perhaps I just went to bed in the hotel.

I do remember the most amazing breakfast the next morning, after a wonderful, jetlag-busting sleep. It was probably down to the fruit platter and how exotic it was for breakfast. The fresh mango was a big factor—very popular in Australia but not what you expected in the early 1990s!

After breakfast, we did some more exploring on the "hop-on hop-off" bus, and I got more out of that. We made a few stops. We also went to a department store to get hats and things, as the sun in Australia can be dangerous. Mum was always good at keeping me right with sun cream and all that. I can't remember all the places we went to. Mum kept a journal, and I'm sure I will have another read of it again at some point. I really do love the memories that travel experiences have; it's great to read these things at least every ten or so years—even better to go back or explore new places near and far!

We then found the bus station, and a really nice café to have something tasty to eat before our four-hour bus journey to Canberra. It was amazing how long it took to clear the suburbs—was interesting though.

However, not long out of Sydney the bus broke down, and it took us a good hour or so before we were back heading for Canberra. Was great to be going to see the Doves, a lovely family we got to know when they were on an exchange swap for a year living in Peebles. We have stayed in touch with them ever since then. It's funny how you can make such good friendships with folk over the relatively short period of a year. Through them visiting the UK, I have caught up with them since this trip, except for the son, Alistair, whom I have not seen since this trip in 1991!

I can remember arriving at the Doves' house to be welcomed by a few stunning blue and red parrots flying in the garden—saw loads of these all over the city, totally weird! I really enjoyed being in Canberra. Catriona and Alistair were around our ages and hosted us really well. The two families did some things together, but quite often the kids would go to the cinema or water park while the adults did something else.

Another memory is that I thought there was a star on top of the Christmas tree, but it started to move, and it was a huge huntsman spider! I was sleeping in the lounge with it for much of my stay there. We got it much later in my time there via some spider spray! I think that spiders were one of my fears about going to Australia!

It was surreal to be having a barbie for Christmas Day lunch by the lake! And going for a swim after the BBQ! A real Aussie thing to do. I loved the popular TV soap *Neighbours*, which was at its UK peak around this time, but that was filmed in Melbourne so we never really had any connection to it while we were there.

At New Year, I was the only person under eighteen, but to all the kids' credit, we decided against going to a bar and just enjoyed the street atmosphere of the city-centre square.

A day or two after New Year, the adults went to

the Snowy Mountains for a few days, leaving the kids in Canberra. We all just played games and went to the cinema. One of the things we went to see was *The Commitments*, which I loved—I've since seen the stage version in the West End in London. We also did a really cool bobsleigh-type thing in the countryside with plastic sleighs on a metal track—I loved this!

It was a sad farewell a few days later. Next, we caught a flight to Cairns and had about a week there. Two highlights in Cairns: one was possibly dyspraxia-related and quite funny but could have gone horribly wrong! We were snorkelling at the Great Barrier Reef—an incredible experience looking at the amazing coloured fish and coral. We were passed around things like sea cucumbers, although my coordination and general inability to do these things well meant I drank half the sea! Back on the boat after an amazing smorgasbord-type lunch, they announced, "Who wants to go boom netting?" (Or something like that!) Me and my sister joined a number of other folk and the boat sped off with us holding onto a waffle-type net. My swimming shorts didn't want to stay on—I'd probably not put them tight enough. Both my sister and the pretty girl next to me helped me keep my modesty just about alive, but it was a very embarrassing situation!

We had some other good days out, including to a drive-in cinema. We had hired a convertible 1970s VW Beetle, which was really cool. Carole was even allowed to drive it! We also went swimming in the sea in a cordoned-off area to protect us from deadly box jellyfish. I also went on a harbour lunch cruise with Dad, and we managed to see some saltwater crocodiles fairly close up. A few days earlier, we had gone to a crocodile farm and Dad had got too close to one behind the barrier and it reacted by flapping about and covering Dad in mud and crocodile poo!

The trip of a lifetime was over; Mum stayed for a few weeks to spend more time with my sister, but it was time for me and Dad to fly back home. Again, I struggled to sleep, and on the fairly long change in Singapore airport, I was totally gone and managed a few hours' sleep on the uncomfortable airport chairs!

I remember getting into Heathrow and, through Dad's British Airways silver or gold card, he managed to get us into the nice airport lounge for an hour or two before our shuttle to Edinburgh.

Greece

My stepsister, Sarah, got married in Greece, and Carole and I joined my dad and his wife, Janice, and my Aunt Betty and Uncle George there along with my stepbrother, Simon. Carole and I stayed at friends' or relatives' of Sarah's husband, Aris, in the city of Thessaloniki.

We had some good nights out before the wedding. I remember going to a whisky club, where the table literally buys a bottle of whisky between everyone. I remember there was a fairly famous Greek female singer, and she was engaging the people in the club by going round the tables while singing and putting the microphone up to a few people to join in the well-known songs. Well, she seemed to think I'd know the song—my tan must have been good, as I don't really think I looked Greek—I think I just sang, "la, la, la!!!" I think some of our table were rolling about the floor in fits of laughter and some were a bit embarrassed!

The wedding was great—a lovely church, so rich in décor with gold there. The meal was amazing—Aris is a chef, and we were at a superb restaurant with an amazing meze never-ending feast!

A day or so after the wedding, we had a day trip to the beach where my aunt and uncle were staying. This was the lovely Halkadiki area. It was nice to spend some time at an amazing beach. I enjoyed a few piña coladas and sunbathing on the sandy beach!

* * *

For the next few years, I didn't go abroad. I had been setting up home in Hawick, had my first mortgage and was getting used to the transition after fully moving out of home. I had quite a few weekends away to lovely places: Carlisle, Lancaster, Preston, Aviemore, Inveraray, the Lake District and Blackpool.

I didn't even have a valid passport for a two- or three-year period! It was only when a workmate suggested a lads' trip to Amsterdam that I organised a passport. It ended up being an almost-full passport, with some amazing trips!

Amsterdam, Netherlands

One of my workmates invited me to join a lads' trip to Amsterdam. At the peak of planning, there were about sixteen of us on the trip, but almost on a daily basis, people started to pull out. I think I was the only single guy in the group! Eventually it was just me going. I had already booked my flights and hotel and just decided to go on my own. I was used to short breaks on my own anyway, as per some of the short weekend breaks I mentioned.

Anyway, it was quite an adventure and my first time going abroad all by myself. I should be grateful to my friend, as this was essentially the trip that really kick-started my interest in travel. It was a great city to explore.

It was such a friendly place, full of interesting museums and experiences—I never did anything too naughty. I did have a space muffin, though, which was allowed there. This had unusual ingredients in it—I never appreciated the ingredients at the start, and perhaps all the questions I was asked were a giveaway! "Do you want a strong, medium or mild muffin?" "Medium, please." "Do you want a whole, half or a quarter muffin?" "A whole one, of course!"

I had the muffin with a coffee, and it tasted quite unusual, not at all unpleasant. I took my time and relaxed for forty-five minutes or so and felt fine after eating it. This was in the late afternoon.

Afterwards, I went for a nice walk by the canals for another forty-five minutes or so. Apart from the muffin, I'd hardly had anything to eat, so when I spotted a table d'hote menu in a French-style restaurant at a reasonable price for early dining, I headed there.

I enjoyed a nice glass of white wine, and it went well with the bread and the starter. After the starter, I started to feel dizzy and ill. The thing about Amsterdam is that most of the buildings are small townhouses, typically over three floors, and, as such, they have spiralling staircases. The toilets were up the stairs. I made it up ok, but the waiters had to help me back down the stairs. I'm sure this has happened to other people before! I think being a tight Scot, I was determined to finish my dinner and, while I struggled to enjoy it like I normally would have, I did finish the meal!

I went back to my hotel and had a wee vomit. After a few hours' sleep, I felt great, so headed back out for a wander enjoying the city's atmosphere and went for a few drinks!

This was a great two-night trip, and I decided I was going to go abroad again at the next opportunity.

Work had been tough going. I had been a manager for a few years but had been stressed about time management issues—essentially, my coordination issues had been picked up on. I had booked a late winter/early spring holiday. This is now almost always the time of year I go abroad, normally a week in the autumn and two weeks in the mid to late winter.

Cyprus

My friend Calum was born in Cyprus, and he suggested it to me. My research was good and, being the bargain hunter I can be, I had found a decent five-star hotel with a good reputation and choice of buffet or à la carte dining (which was especially good for me as I don't really like buffet set-ups) for only £499, with the first two weeks half-board and the third week on a bed and breakfast basis. This was in the outskirts of Limassol. I put the hotel to Calum, who had been there himself, and he told me it was a good choice. It was indeed a good choice! I had a lovely room— while only half-board, the drinks were a good price, especially considering it was five-star. There was a complimentary fruit bowl and bottle of local wine on arrival. I knew that public transport was quite poor, so I had booked lots of excursions, seven or eight, and spread them out, so there was a good mix of my own arrangements and excursions.

This was a nice trip, and I actually exercised

well, as I walked into the city, which was about four miles each way!

Staying the three weeks was probably a bit much, and I was maybe a bit bored towards the middle of the second week. Then I had a brainwave! I had seen local travel agents advertising trips to Egypt. They were mainly day trips, but I decided this was too much for one day and asked at my hotel about overnight trips, as I recalled Calum mentioning a mini-cruise on an ancient Louis Cruise Lines ship. The mini-cruises were not running until the following month.

I went round a few travel agents who had deals for three-night trips to Cairo in the window, and all were a bit abrupt with me, telling me of course they couldn't offer me this. I even said I knew a single would cost more, but none were prepared to look into it for me.

I thought I would try one more travel agent. A really nice lady welcomed me, understood the deal, and with a five-minute phone call could offer me the deal for just a small supplement—sorted!

A few days later I was at Larnaka airport, about to have a holiday within a holiday! When we landed at Cairo, the tour operator met me and I was introduced to the rest of the British people who had booked the trip. There was myself and three other couples, all friendly folk. Two couples were at the Marriott, one couple was at the Hilton and, just to be different, I was at the independent Ramses hotel (or something like that!). I liked my hotel—it was traditional and charming, slightly old-fashioned. So cheap, had a fairly basic à la carte dinner, was nothing exciting but a really good price. I did, however, really enjoy the Egyptian red wine I had alongside it!

It was really hard to sleep as vehicle horns were going off all the time. You could almost tell the time of day by how many horns you heard each hour! Being an older hotel meant that it didn't have good enough soundproof glazing! I woke up a bit tired but looking forward to seeing the great sights. Over the next few days, we went to the pyramids, the Sphinx, the great museum where the mummies are and an evening River Nile city cruise. It was a great few days, and then I went back to Cyprus for the last few days of the three-week trip. During this stay, I also managed to whack my head on a street sign; I think all the noise issues had disturbed me a bit. Thankfully I had no obvious problems as a result. A passerby did ask if I was ok!

Overall, this was a great trip. I had tried to meet up with Calum, who was coincidentally staying in another part of the island, but we both had communication issues, and these were the days before mobiles were really mainstream.

Reflecting on this trip and thinking about the next trip, I really enjoyed the side trip to Egypt and didn't think I would enjoy the likes of a package trip to a Spanish island or anything like that. I felt that those sort of trips are more family targeted, and I would look to do more unusual options.

I had dial-up internet at home, which was still a bit of a luxury back then. I was just about able to get into some sort of travel website that was offering deals for luxury Dubai hotels at really good prices. Yes, this all seemed interesting, and was my next choice!

Dubai

The Glasgow service with Emirates didn't exist at this time, but I have heard this is an amazing airline.

I picked up the London Gatwick service. Again, I'd looked for a balance of hotel quality and price. I stayed at the Dubai Marine Beach resort and spa. I was in a mini-suite, had great facilities and marble everywhere. The only bad thing was that the family in the neighbouring apartment seemed to be night animals and every night without fail, between one and three in the morning, their kid would spend two hours banging things and running up and down the communal stairs. The parents were not interested. I did complain to them and should have complained to the hotel manager to at least get a move to a quieter apartment. I'm better at these things nowadays!

On this trip, around 2002, Dubai was a very different place, probably half the size or less than it is today. The world's only seven-star hotel, Burj Arab, was open and very close to my hotel, but most of the hotels there today were just a thought back then. I remember going to a shopping mall and being in awe of the look of it and the wealth.

It was the hottest time to be in Dubai. Temperatures reached around fifty degrees centigrade! It wasn't as bad as you would think, especially swimming in the clear blue sea and sitting at the beach. I did a city tour and also a jeep safari, but the jeep safari wasn't really my thing.

The food was amazing. It was my first time trying Lebanese and I loved the healthiness of this. I enjoyed some hubba bubba pipe smoking—a real novelty! There was also an amazing Italian restaurant and a specific fine dining place. Prices were great value back then; it's changed quite a lot since then and is more premium these days. It's a very interesting place to go to.

* * *

After this trip, I had my round-the-world trip, which I have written a journal about and cover in a separate chapter. Then there were a lot of cruises, which again I cover in another chapter, and same with the travel industry trips.

Therefore, we are fast-forwarding a number of years.

Malta

I went to Malta a few years ago and enjoyed it so much that I went back a year later. I still enjoyed it, so I went back two years later! I stayed at the same all-inclusive hotel each time, the Seabank.

First time I went, I loved it. I really enjoyed Malta as a whole. Valetta is a really nice city with a lot of history. Rabat/Medina is a stunning fortified town and is where a lot of the programme *Game of Thrones* was filmed. Bugibba has a great motor museum and an aquarium.

I liked the all-inclusive hotel, especially the Italian restaurant (which was not as good the second and third stays) and the Brazilian one where the meat was carved at your table. There was also a jungle (American restaurant) and a few Maltese buffet-type ones.

The rooms were also a real draw, a really high standard, and it was all good value. I felt the rooms were really strong four-star standard.

It had a nice spa and treatments were good value. Despite being a bloke, I do enjoy having a spa treatment. The indoor pool was good the first time, ok the second, and way too busy my last time.

I was also made to feel special during my second stay with a repeat-guest afternoon tea, which was really good and encouraged me to book a third time! On my third stay, I never had anything offered like that and I also ended up moving rooms due to an issue with the toilet not flushing and a lack of urgency for them sorting this. The hotel dynamic has changed and become much more family-orientated. I would say it's not a hotel I would go back to for a fourth time.

Turkey

In between my second and third trips to Malta, I had a trip to Turkey. This was a two-centre trip to a supposed five-star hotel in Alanya and then to a boutique hotel in central Istanbul.

Firstly, Turkish Airlines were amazing, one of the best economy services I've ever had. The Edinburgh-Istanbul flight must be one of the shortest flights with seatback TV and decent choice of movies. The food was outstanding—I would easily say the best economy food I've had. Qantas and Emirates are also excellent with economy food, but Turkish is slightly better!

I had a long connection wait in the domestic terminal in Istanbul and was not that impressed with this terminal—very limited offerings. I had a short late-evening flight, then a ninety-minute drive to the resort.

I had a really bad first impression at the Titan Select hotel. When I arrived, they had overbooked, and I was to be downgraded to the four-star Titan Garden hotel for the first night. There was no apology about the issue, I was given a sandwich and water and was taken via the staff quarters, which were horrible and rundown and gave a very poor impression. My old-fashioned room was not good—it seemed clean but just stuck in a time warp—also there was just a very thin sheet on what was meant to be a king-sized bed. The hotel was aware I was going to arrive about midnight, so my room should have been kept. The sheet was no good, and there seemed to be a lot of love-making going on in the surrounding bedrooms! I was given a blanket, but the situation was still far from ideal and way too noisy. I went back, saying it was not acceptable, and they "found" a room at the hotel I was meant to be in. The abrupt receptionist demanded the room back the next day. It smelled bad, but I was shattered, it had a proper duvet and everything, and would be ok for the night.

I slept through breakfast, and eventually got up, mainly due to housekeeping trying to kick me out. I showered, and there was a major issue with the drain—this was the source of the smell. It was disgusting. I went downstairs and found Guest Relations, who told me she would sort a suitable room, apologised and offered me a free hammam massage experience as an apology. She told me to go to the spa after a few hours and I could book the massage. She also told me she would meet me in an hour to show me my new room.

I was unhappy with the new room as I had booked a room with a king bed and this was a twin room. I showed her my confirmation, and she said that it was a mistake, as they don't book single people into king rooms. Again I got my way, although she changed and was less friendly and more reluctant to help.

I didn't like the food or the à la carte—the one free meal per stay never transpired. The two à la carte restaurants were rarely open, and when they actually were, I was told I couldn't use them. Occasionally, birds flew into the restaurants, and there were a few flies and cats. I didn't find this good.

The beach wasn't great; there was a pretty basic burger restaurant there. I did actually like one of the bars at the neighbouring hotel that I was able to use.

I did a few sightseeing trips. I really liked the boat trip. In fact, I enjoyed it so much I did it twice! It took us to great sea-swimming places and was good fun with ok food. Nicely organised, it was more for younger folk, but I did enjoy it.

I also went on a quad bike safari. There was a mini obstacle course, and the organiser was in two minds about letting me do the main thing and he suggested I could be a passenger on his larger quad! I told him no way, unless I was taken back to the hotel immediately and given a refund. He told me that was not possible, and then allowed me to do the quad bike course. I was not diagnosed as dyspraxic at this stage, and the guy's concern was probably fair.

I did just about manage the quad. It was quite a challenging circuit, through a big stream, almost a river, and there were quite a lot of twists and turns. I would say I'm good at driving cars, but that's definitely at the upper end of my capabilities. The girl behind me actually bumped her quad into mine twice. I told her off and suggested that she should go ahead of me to avoid this happening again. I enjoyed this activity but was actually glad when it came to an end!

I went on a trip to the historic small city of Side. I found a nice wee independent travel agent to book the excursions through, and they were all less than £30. The Side one included a lunch as well. I was the only British person, and there was a Russian and German guide who had very limited English skills and was a bit abrupt when addressing me. The places were interesting, and I guess despite the lack of suitable guides it was an ok experience.

My last trip was to a traditional hammam for a full Turkish massage experience. This was really good. The lady who ran the place was really kind with me and explained the processes really well. There was a sauna, a mud bath, a rock salt room, and a fish spa, which I did go into! The main foam massage was done in a steam room. This was a great experience and was good value.

The second-to-last night of this part of the holiday, I became really unwell. I was so sick at both ends of my body, it was the worst food poisoning I ever had. The hotel offered a private ambulance to a private hospital; I declined this and, via a taxi, was able to find a twenty-four-hour pharmacy, which gave me really good medication. My biggest worry was if I would be able to make the short flight the next day from Alanya to Istanbul. Thankfully, I did feel a bit better and did manage the transfer to the airport, but was glad of the stop halfway to the airport. On arrival, I felt well enough to drink two freshly-squeezed orange juices that seemed to get my vitamin levels back.

I hadn't booked a transfer to the hotel but came across a very helpful lady at a desk who sorted everything, and while the drive took a good hour or so, with some relief I started to feel a lot better. It was a nice but long drive in, as we had landed at the other airport, interestingly the Asia-based one.

Istanbul is uniquely in two continents, part in Europe and part in Asia. It is a stunning city and rich in culture. I couldn't have been happier when I arrived at my lovely boutique hotel. It really was a stunning little hotel. My room was tastefully decorated with lovely antique knicknacks. The hotel was a few side streets away from the main areas, only a five- or ten-minute walk to some of the nicest sights like the Blue Mosque. Because it was in a quiet cul-de-sac, it wasn't noisy. I was almost one hundred percent better when I got to the hotel, but once I checked in, I went to bed for a few hours, trying to recover from the lack of sleep and no longer fearing that I was about to be sick!

When I felt better, I went to a hubba bubba café and started with a Coke to drink—wasn't ready for alcohol yet! I loved the smell there of the different flavours of smoking tobacco, though I wasn't ready for that tonight. This was to be a two-night stay, so I had an early night and was now really looking forward to the next few days.

I was so pleased with the medication. The next morning, I was totally better and enjoyed a nice continental breakfast at the lovely garden café in the hotel. I was ready to explore the city.

First, I went to the Grand Bazaar and mainly bought loose-leaf tea and some other bits and bobs. It was a great experience, and the bazaar seemed to go on forever.

What wasn't so good were the street sellers. One of these pestered me a few times. He acknowledged the previous times he had spoken to me too! He said he had a souvenir shop close by. A customer was just leaving as I arrived; my arrival probably helped them with leaving. Again, I was offered a drink and refused, as then you almost feel obliged to buy something, and they insisted I have a drink. Drink arrived, then they put the blinds down and locked the door. Not at all happy then, and I will never make the same mistake a third time, as the same thing had happened in Egypt! There was nothing I wanted to buy, and it was a hard and uncomfortable sales process. I stuck to my guns and managed to get them to let me out. That put a sour end to my mostly enjoyable shopping experience.

I then grabbed a nice traditional mixed kebab meal in an outdoor café very close to my hotel. It was great value. It was great to enjoy a traditional, tasty meal just hours after not being able to stomach food!

I then did the "hop-on hop-off" bus—really enjoyable in this fascinating city. This took about three hours. Back to the hotel for a shower, then out for dinner.

I picked what looked like the nicest restaurant and this one had a special toughened glass floor at certain parts so you could look into the historic stone basement. The food was great, and the Turkish Chardonnay was exotic and had that lovely buttery flavour to it.

After dinner I went back to the hubba bubba café and enjoyed a fruit liquid tobacco. I opted for Turkish Delight flavour, and it's such a relaxing thing to do. I had done this before in Dubai and it was great.

After my final breakfast, I paid a compliment to the guy at the hotel desk; turned out he was the owner, and he was delighted with my feedback and offered me a Turkish coffee, which I really enjoyed, but just at this time my transfer bus arrived. I would definitely go on another city break here, using the amazing Turkish Air service from Edinburgh.

Apart from my third visit to Malta, this was the last non-cruise holiday for me. I tend to mainly cruise these days, but in February 2019, I have my first ever trip to Las Vegas to look forward to!

CHAPTER 8

My First Round-The-World Trip
Around the World in Twenty-Two Days

Edinburgh – (London Heathrow) – Singapore – Perth – Ayers Rock – Sydney – Melbourne – Sydney – Christchurch – Auckland – Los Angeles – New York – (London Heathrow) – Edinburgh

16/2/2006
True to my responsibility as a Team Manager, I'm not out sharp as I stay on to finish my batch of ten pieces of correspondence. At least I'm thanked by my boss, Dave.

Also, a colleague wound me up with some phone call pretending to be from the airline, telling me my flight is cancelled! I do see the funny side, but I'm in a really good mood, although a bit nervous about such a big trip. The thought I'm about to travel around the world is really exciting!

Weird thing happened at work today. I bumped into my old college friend Roddy, not seen him in around ten years, he is also a manager. Roddy is one of the good guys and I'm now looking forward to going for a pint with him when I get back from my big trip!

18:10 – I book a taxi for 18:30, much better than getting buses etc. Mum offered to take me, but as she is picking me up at the end of the trip, I am more than happy to make my own way to the Quality Hotel Edinburgh airport hotel.

19:15 – After settling into my hotel room have an average dinner, but at a rate of £50 for dinner and B&B can't complain!

20:45 – Alarm call booked for 5am, never mind! That's life for the fussy round-the-world traveller. No budget airlines for me—flying British Airways, Qantas and American Airlines.

My travel agent would not book my return flights to Melbourne as they can't believe I would consider paying an extra $20 to go with Qantas rather than the budget airline, Virgin Blue, who are quite like EasyJet.

17/2/2006
Here we are. Not many people go around the world in twenty-two days!

04:45 – Got up early despite alarm set for 5am—too excited! Everything is going to plan. Hardly slept last night worrying about not getting up in time.

06:15 – British Airways check-in assistant very helpful. I find myself fully checked in for my Qantas flight to Singapore. This will save me so much time as I only have just over two hours to turnabout at Heathrow.

09:00 – At Heathrow Terminal 1, only takes about thirty minutes to go through the security formalities and get to Terminal 4, meaning I end up with a relaxing hour to browse the airport shops before my flight is called.

10:30 – My flight is called—this is it! My last experience of long-haul was ok apart from a lack of sleep.

12 noon – Flight departs about thirty minutes late, which is fine. I didn't realise how crap the leg room is! This is reduced to almost zero when the man in front of me put his chair back as far as it reclines—nightmare! He does this for the whole flight apart from when he eats! Hope I don't get deep-vein whatdoyoucallit?!

12:30 – A nice glass of Aussie sparkling wine! Also, while I remember, it's now sort of 20:30 as I put my watch forward immediately, which makes it easier to identify time going by.

18/2/2006

03:00 – Bored, can't sleep and sore leg due to lack of foot room! Watch TV for a bit, try to sleep but can't.

06:00 – Breakfast and under two hours until landing in Singapore!

08:00 – Land at Singapore! It's a beautiful morning and a comfortable temperature of about twenty-five degrees! What a lovely and efficient airport—spotless! My luggage is on the carousel immediately. My friendly driver gives me a warm welcome and takes me to the Summerview Hotel.

09:00 – Arrive at the Summerview Hotel. The friendly receptionist checks me in and yay! My room is ready! Not meant to check in until 1 p.m., so already a massive thumbs-up! Room is ok, good value at about £34 a night B&B at a three-star hotel.

16:30 – I wake up after a good six-hour jet-lag recovery sleep, feel quite refreshed. Read over touristy things, go to reception, who kindly book me a city tour for 9 a.m. tomorrow. There is no Raffles hotel tour on Sunday, but I will go on my own and see what dining options there are tomorrow afternoon. Mum had an amazing afternoon tea here!

Reading through my touristy stuff is good as I find out my hotel is fairly central, and it seems a fairly easy city to get about.

Decide that I'm now feeling up to a wander about to explore the local area. I'm near a market/bazaar, which is interesting. I just have a browse, all good to look at but nothing I want/need to buy. I pass an interesting temple.

18:30 – This was my sister Carole's tip and it's a good one—thanks, Sis! This is to go to a food hall, a bit like the ones in some of our shopping centres. This is a treat and is full of locals (always a good sign)! First meal on land is a crayfish noodle soup. Meal was about £1.40 and was massive, a main course and not a starter! Glad I wasn't greedy like normal!

After dinner, I take another wander, then go to another café for a dessert of mixed fruit ice with a milk/yogurt sauce, sherbet, fresh fruit cubes—kiwi, mango and strawberry—mango syrup and mango sorbet. At £2.50, this is dearer than my main course but is a great treat!

I then grab a can of beer from a twenty-four-hour store, and some sun cream.

I head back to the hotel and write this up. It's now 21:30 and it's time for bed. I'm nowhere near as tired as I was when I went to Australia as a teenager. I would say that a stopover in long-haul travel is a must, and my first impressions of Singapore are great!

19/2/2006

06:50 – Get up early as I can't sleep. Breakfast at 07:20 is adequate but basic—at least it's all included. The restaurant staff don't speak any English. Eventually my "give us a clue" sketch of "where's the milk/sugar" seems to work! The staff are a bit grumpy/can't be bothered, but never mind!

08:50 – My city tour is true to Singapore form and is very punctual—ten minutes early! It's a minibus with just me—help! I hope I've not been kidnapped! Mum had a scary, funny story of her city tour, so I knew what to expect and can see where she was coming from. A few more people eventually get on at other hotels and shortly we arrive at a coach station where we meet the main bus. City tour guide is ok, quite enthusiastic but speaks at a thousand miles per hour! Seems to also go between Chinese and English very quickly. I catch some information but not everything, this sentence will come back to punish me!

The sights are interesting, but the stops are wrong—either too long with nothing to do (e.g. a jewellery factory) or too short (e.g. botanical gardens)! We arrive at the huge gardens and only have thirty minutes unguided. I enjoy a wander and, ten minutes before we are due to leave, I go to the pick-up point. Loads of buses and reps are here. I ask if all the coaches stop here. Yes, they all say confidently, so I wait. Eventually the pick-up time passes. I panic and now decide to run to the starting point. It's about thirty-three degrees Celsius today, so a good one-kilometre run must lose me a stone through sweat—yuck! Bus is there with everyone else. I apologise as I'm fifteen minutes late, hot and distressed. I'm told no big deal and not to worry!

2pm – Having got back to the hotel, I take a cool bath. I decide to go to the Raffles hotel for afternoon tea. As it's Sunday, there are no tours. I make my own way there. I attempt to go by rickshaw, but they only seem to be picking up locals, same with the taxis. Eventually I manage to get one. It only costs about £1.60. On arriving at this stunning hotel—one of the nicest hotels on the planet!—I walk around some of the hotel shops and try to get afternoon tea; however, only informal bars appear to be open, I think because it's a Sunday. I go to one of the bars and have a Singapore Sling at the hotel that invented this refreshing cocktail! I manage to find the underground train back to my hotel, which is modern, and the trains are fully air-conditioned. There are three proper lines and another two lines that are just one stop long. It's efficient and impressive, although it's so busy and feels much busier than the London Underground! It's not a patch on my favourite District line—old, historic and smelly (*although the District line has since been upgraded*)!

After getting back to the hotel, I relax for an hour before heading to Chinatown. The tour guide said this was a one-hundred-percent must-do place to go for dinner. The restaurant I chose wasn't cheap, but there were some cheap places. I mainly made my choice as I wanted to sit inside an air-conditioned place, and most of the cheaper places were outdoor courtyard-type places.

6pm – It's about thirty degrees C. I find somewhere that appears to be an authentic Chinese buffet where the choices are brought to you. It's busy—as before, this is a good sign. As I said, it's a place where you choose about eight different dishes and they bring the raw food with a mini personal cooker. (This is known as Chinese hot-pot, and my ex-girlfriend Lucy treated me to this in Edinburgh when I got back from my trip!)

Typical Michael!—I choose really weird stuff such as sea cucumber, Chinese melon (not sweet), unusual meat. I don't have a clue how to cook the things, what to cook and what to eat raw, much to the amusement of the restaurant staff! I soon discover that I'm meant to cook everything! They amuse themselves for a bit, but then rescue me just before I'm about to poison myself! It's a bit of a disaster; however, I would have regretted not going to the real Chinatown, so no regrets! I should have asked Lucy more about this before I left the UK! It costs about $50 Singapore dollars which works out at about £20. I could have had about ten meals from last night for about this cost, but it did include three Tiger (Singapore) beers so I can't complain. So much cheaper than back in the UK!

I decide that after breakfast tomorrow I will go to the zoo. I need to be back at the hotel for 16:45 to catch my airport transfer. Anyway, it's 22:30 and time for bed. I think that Perth is actually in the same time zone, although I don't arrive there until about 00:30, which will probably mean that it'll be after 01:30 by the time I get to my Perth hotel. Anyway, goodnight!

20/6/2006

09:00 – I have a lie-in until around 9 a.m. and grab another ok breakfast that is a mixture of Asian and Western food including rice, noodles, eggs, mini sausages and chips! Also, some nice fresh fruit, horrible fruit juice, more like diluting juice, and coffee.

10:00 – I have packed all my luggage and left it at reception for collection at 16:30.

Decided to go to the zoo. Singapore has one of the best zoos in the world. Probably not as many animals as London, but a bigger area, which gives the animals more freedom—the idea is to give the animals more space and keep it as natural as possible. I was tempted to have an organised trip to the zoo; this would have cost three times as much but included having breakfast with an orangutan! I decide not to do this to save money. I really enjoy walking around the zoo for a few hours, but it is so hot and humid and is very hard work. They have a number of air-conditioned shelters that allow you to escape the hot weather for a bit. These are good to step into, especially as it is around 40 degrees!

The public transport works out well, although there is some misunderstanding with a bus driver who doesn't speak any English. It takes about an hour and a half each way, and the round trip costs the equivalent of about £2. All the buses are air-conditioned.

15:30 – I get back at my hotel with just over an hour until my airport transfer is due. I decide to do three things:

1 - I buy a weird ice cream. The choices were strange, chili and sweetcorn to name a few. I can't remember the type I chose, but once the wrapper was removed, it smelt horrible and tasted even worse, but only cost about 40p!

2 – I grab a large cool Tiger beer, this is really refreshing. It's ice-cold and they almost always serve it in a frosted glass. This is a 660ml bottle so is almost a pint and a half!

3 – I check my emails at an internet café next to the hotel, although the PC is very slow.

Overall Singapore has been a great experience, very different culturally. At least the locals aren't not in-your-face like some other countries. I would like to come back here as there are still some other things I would like to do. I also wouldn't like to go non-stop to Australia or New Zealand, especially on economy.

18:00 – The airport goes well. I grab a fresh orange, then later a bottle of water. I'm very tired from all the walking and the heat today, so I do some reading to pass the time.

Flight is thirty minutes late due to a very strange incident. Plane is literally ready to go, even to the point of thrusting its engines, when all of a sudden, the furious pilot announces there is a missing passenger who has just shown up. He goes on to say that it was the airport and not the airline who mucked up and, as the passenger's luggage has been checked into the plane, he has to go back to the terminal. I was not so bothered, although this meant it was not until about 3 a.m. that I got to my hotel.

21/2/2006
01:30 – Arrive at Perth airport, which is very tight on security but low on staff. I can understand that, as who would want to work so late (*irony is I now work this time five days a week*)! Typical of Australian hospitality, I notice immediately that the airport staff are very friendly and welcoming.

I forgot to say that the landing was an experience, as it was very windy and a very rough landing, but the pilot dealt well with the conditions! It's also thirty-two degrees C in the middle of the night!

07:00 – Despite only having about four hours' sleep, I'm actually wide awake and ready to go! I have a very pleasant breakfast. This is a nice little friendly hotel, Sullivan's three-star, really friendly staff. I book a tour for tomorrow, which is a day boat trip to Fremantle. Included is wine tasting. There are alternative excellent lunch/dinner trips, but I feel my tour is best from a tourist perspective, as the other options don't give as much time in Fremantle. Fremantle, I'm told, is a totally "must go to" place. This trip is $34AUD, which then was the equivalent of about £15, really good value.

11:00 – I wander into Perth, maybe should have got a bus. It's forty-three degrees, the hottest day of the year! It's reasonably easy to cope—better than Singapore, as it's a very dry heat. I need a beer though—any excuse! Mmmmm, nice and refreshing! I wander about the city centre, grab an ice cream, then manage to find the on/off tourist tram bus around Perth. This has a laid-back and friendly driver commentary. The cost is comparable with the UK although was better quality, one of the best on/off tours I've had. Perth is a nice city, although two days will be enough.

16:00 – Back at the hotel, grab another pint. Also book my airport bus. I then phone Michelle, whom I used to work with in Edinburgh. She has been living in Australia for about a year. I arrange to meet her for dinner tomorrow in a typical Aussie pub!

18:30 – Dine in the hotel, meal was nice, seafood theme as there often is with me. Fresh sardines to start with and shark for main. Shark is a popular/ common fish course in Oz. Western Australia has the second most shark attacks, behind Florida. The last time I had shark was back in 1991 during my last trip to Australia. I enjoyed it more last time; it's often battered with chips and eaten much like we have cod or haddock in the UK. I enjoy a nice Australian sparkling wine with dinner tonight. It was one of the cheapest bottles on the list. I left about a glass' worth in the bottle (not deliberately). So friendly and helpful are the staff that they phone me to see if I want the rest—yes please!

22/2/2006

Up at just after 7 a.m. because I feel like it! I think in warm countries like this, you often go to bed early then get up early. I enjoy a leisurely breakfast, hand my trousers in to reception to be dry-cleaned, put on sun cream and, before I know it, it's time to get my bus to the pier for my trip to Freo, as the locals call it.

Fremantle is a lovely seaside port stacked with history. When I complete my boat trip to Freo, I get on another mock tram for a tour around here. There is arguably more to do here than in Perth. Certainly more that appeals to my taste. After the mock tram (another of these land train things), I grab a lovely seafood basket lunch that contains loads of different battered seafood with chips and salad. It goes nicely with a Coke. It only costs the equivalent of about £5. I then go around a nice little motor museum with some impressive and historic cars, including a one-time land speed record vehicle and also one of Sir Jackie Stewart's world championship Formula 1 cars.

I then go to the maritime museum where I see

two boats that would really impress my Dad. One is Australian and won the Americas cup in 1983, the first non-American boat to win it in decades. I can't remember the name of the other boat or skipper, but he was an Australian guy who went around the world non-stop three times altogether! It's not even a huge boat, maybe thirty-five or forty feet in length max. I take a couple of photos—hopefully they will come out ok.

I then have a quick beer before rejoining the boat for the return journey. The Swan River is beautiful and large. I spot loads of wildlife such as black swans, storks, flamingos, and I think also a whale, although most people think it's a dolphin. As the Swan River joins the sea, there are often dolphin and whale spottings. Same with sharks, as per my dinner last night! There's also wine tasting, which is good.

When I get back to the pier, my problem is getting a taxi to meet up with my friend Michelle. After twenty minutes, eventually I get one. I'm fifteen minutes late. Michelle jokingly tells me off, and I apologise big-time—I hate being late! I also remind her (also jokingly) that she was sometimes late at work when I used to be her boss! Her flatmate Terry was also a former workmate, and he joins us for thirty minutes before he goes off to work. Michelle and I then have a nice meal in a trendy but good value restaurant. I have blueback crab omelette, which is really nice; Michelle has a nice steak. We talk about the old times working in Edinburgh, as she calls it, in the "gas chambers". She has done well for herself and is now an HR manager at a department store and is on an extended visa, likely to become an Australian citizen within the next six months (*this happened*). I go back to her apartment for an after-dinner tea. She even has a shared outdoor swimming pool. She doesn't have air-con though, which can be quite an issue in the hot Western Australian weather.

I get a taxi back to the hotel and pack most of my stuff before bed. It's now 22:30.

23/2/2006
06:30 – Early start as my airport bus is due at 07:30. Having an hour gives me plenty of time to get sorted and checked out of the hotel. It's been a nice stay in a good hotel in a great Australian city.

I can't remember if I said, but a fact about Perth is it has the world's largest botanical gardens— approximately a thousand acres! They cover about a third of the city!

07:30 – Airport bus is bang on time. It only takes us about thirty minutes to do all the pick-ups and arrive at the airport. No queue at the friendly check-in desk. As I have what I think is a two-hour wait, coupled with the fact I didn't have any breakfast at the hotel this morning, I find a nice place and have a tasty breakfast over an hour or so. I then go to an internet place for twenty minutes. I send an email to thank Michelle for meeting me and another email to Keith, whom I also worked with, funnily enough in the same team as Michelle! He now lives in Sydney and is married to an Australian lady, Amy. Hopefully I will meet up with him.

10:00 – Plane is called for boarding, then 10:05 boarding is cancelled with everyone sent back to the terminal.

10:10 – We are informed that our elderly Boeing 717 has a small fuel leak. This reminds me of our family trip years ago on Yugoslav airline Adria Airways!

10:40 – We board again and will be at least thirty minutes late. We sit on the plane for thirty minutes to be told that there is still a problem! Should be ok soon but will have to go back to the terminal. We see technicians around.

12:30 – Finally take off over two hours late, but to be fair on Qantas, we got free refreshments during our extended wait.

Interesting landscape out of the window on our flight of vast red/brown desert land. Even the farms are more grey than green due to severe droughts. I'm really looking forward to Ayers Rock. Mum and Carole recently asked what I'm most looking forward to—I answered Ayers Rock.

Flying over Ayers Rock prior to landing is impressive. I can see the shadows, and it's easy to understand the historical importance of this area.

It's a tiny wee airport, with limited facilities.

I grab the hotel bus. I get to see the outside of all the hotels, as mine is furthest away. Reception is quite nice and, for what it is, my lodge-style room is a good size and is clean.

I go to reception to check on tour times and am disappointed to discover that only one out of three restaurants at my hotel is open. All over the hotel are signs saying *Keep out – refurbishment!* I complain to reception as the only restaurant that is open is a DIY BBQ place—good fun with other people but not really an "on your own" type of place. I'm offered a free DIY breakfast, but I decline the offer and ask for a move to another hotel that has the facilities I am expecting. On reflection, from a dyspraxic point of view, this set-up of unfamiliar DIY cooking isn't really suitable. I get offered a non-subsidised upgrade for £130. I refuse and am told my only option is to contact my UK travel agent saying that I should have been told about the refurbishment. I counter-argue this by reminding them their website has no information on the refurbishment. They agree and state it's a costing issue, but all the people who book should have been told. She gets quite grumpy; eventually I very reluctantly agree to email my travel agent but am annoyed how this has been handled.

I mope about for a bit but also feel that I have overreacted a bit. I think part of it was trying to blag a better room with a bathroom, although you do get used to the lack of facilities.

Resort is quite lively/youthful, or my lodge hotel is anyway. I go to the hotel viewport of Ayers Rock, and it is some place! Loads of insects all over, including in my room—nothing I can't handle though!

I check with reception about a few restaurants, but everything I like the sound of is shut! I end up back at the DIY BBQ, which has emu, and crocodile sausages/skewers. I am adventurous and choose a mixed pack, giving me a taste of everything. You get a free salad bar with your food, which is ok. I have to cook myself and manage ok, and it's quite nice although it is a bit busy and I don't really like the communal BBQ. I do talk to a Scottish couple from Kirriemuir—never heard of it! I enjoy a nice beer alongside the food. There is also some entertainment. After the meal, I have an early night at 20:30 and set the alarm for 04:30!

24/2/06
04:30 – I wake up and get up fine. Have a reasonable shower in the shared block and take

my time getting ready. It's pretty comfortable weather this time in the morning.

05:45 – Get picked up and off to the camel farm. The guide is a real Crocodile Dundee character who tells good stories. Turns out all his camels were wild ones. An interesting fact is that there are one million wild camels in Australia, and it's the only country in the world with wild camels. I meet my new buddy, Sally the camel. I am the first in our group to get on a camel, and she is actually the last camel in the line—This pleased me as I got to see all the camels in front of me.

While I have been on several camels before—in UAE, Egypt and Cyprus—I have never had a proper go, and this is for a good hour or perhaps even an hour and a half. We have lovely views of the rock as well, and also Kata Jura, the other interesting rock formation, which I don't have time to visit during my short stay here. Also heard the amazing sound of dingoes barking as the sun rose. Never saw them but hearing them was great!

After the trek through a small patch of the desert is finished, we get some nice Billy tea and beer bread. Billy tea is, erm…just like tea with tea leaves in it. There is probably more to it than that. Beer bread is good though, has a slight cheesy flavour to it. The friendly owner then shows us around the farm, where we see baby camels etc. The one-hour tour ends up being about three hours. There are nice people in our group who all share travel stories.

Get dropped back about 08:30, decide to go for a snooze. Before I know it, it's twelve noon. This is not a bad thing though, as I have probably not had huge sleeps, what with early starts and so on.

When I get up, I check my emails, and my travel

agency has been in touch to say I can upgrade for free to a choice of two hotels within the resort. However, the hotel manager is not aware of this and asks me to email him. I do so but he does not receive the email I forward. I reluctantly agree just to stay in the room, on the basis that I will get something knocked off when I get home. I do find the hotel issues frustrating. This hotel cost double the amount of any other nightly rate in my trip (due to the same owner owning all the resort hotels), and I don't even have a toilet and half the facilities are shut! I decide however to forget about the issues and focus on enjoying the rest of my stay here and, to do so, I get booked into a seafood restaurant tonight, which at the time of writing my diary, is the best restaurant in the resort. Since writing this book, however, there is now an amazing outdoor dining experience called the "Sounds of Silence" where it's like a pop-up restaurant in the middle of nowhere to enjoy the views and the sounds. With a decent currency rate for pound sterling to Australian dollar, my meal costs around £20, which is a good price.

13:00 – I go for a swim and share the pool with about a dozen hovering, massive, colourful dragonflies who fly about a millimetre above the water! While I cope with them, they do freak me out a bit. It's a nice pool, a reasonable size and not too busy. This is my first swim of the trip, as, while there was a pool in my Perth hotel, I just never had time to use it.

14:00 – I grab a beer. They have a lovely dark ale, Carlton Black, for about £1.30. It reminded me of my favourite, now extinct, beer, called Gillespie's. I spend an hour or so writing up this diary, then I go to put on more sun cream as I will shortly be going on a three-and-a-half-hour Ayers Rock base tour!

15:30 – Ayers Rock is amazing and very interesting. However, so much is secret. Our guide claims not to know much about it, though. The rock is not as symmetrical as I thought it would be. Every crack or odd shape has a meaning, although we don't get to hear a detailed explanation of this. We pull the bus into an area set up with some tables and chairs to watch the sunset on the rock while drinking some sparkling wine. It's lovely and I do hope the photos turn out (*this trip was really in the days before we had digital cameras and only had basic mobile phones that you could really only use to call, text or, if you were lucky, play Snake*)!

I get back to the hotel just before 20:00. Again, the Aussie, laid-back experience shows. This was meant to be a three-and-a-half-hour trip but lasted about an hour longer than scheduled, which was good as the aura of the rock was amazing. Never climbed the rock, and while I could have, the local community find it disrespectful for people to climb it. It is also difficult to climb, despite having a handrail. It's very steep.

20:00 – Enjoy dinner in the five-star hotel, which is a buffet and is good value. Starter of oysters, prawns in the shells, octopus, mussels—all the things I love eating! Pretty ordinary mains and desserts, but amazing starters! With drinks, the meal is about £30, which is really good! (*I have just checked the prices now and they are a lot dearer, as expected.*)

22:00 – Grab another Carlton Black beer and listen to some traditional music at my hotel's outdoor bar before bed. Meant to say that Aboriginal people are often in my bar. Interesting to hear them talk in their own unique language.

25/2/06

08:30 – Get up and shower and pack. Ayers Rock has been an experience. I will miss a lot about it but will also appreciate no longer having to use a horrible communal shower block and smelly communal toilet block.

11:00 – First Qantas plane to take off on time. If you want alcohol you have to pay, which was a first for my Qantas trips. Happy to have a good old Coke instead.

15:30 – Arrive in Sydney, get an airport bus, and despite the driver and ticket man managing to offend half the passengers, I find them quite funny—they're like Laurel and Hardy! I get to my hotel, The Unilodge, in reasonable time.

My hotel room is quite different, it's a sort of mini-suite. It's quite small, but as per all the hotels, I have a nice double bed!

17:00 – I arrive at Circular Quay, which is right by the famous Harbour Bridge and Opera House. It brings back memories. I take a nostalgic meal in City Extra, which is a twenty-four-hour diner-type café/bar/restaurant that I remember going to as a seventeen-year-old on the special holiday with my family. It's not the same. My biggest issue is that the main course arrives halfway through my starter. This has happened a few times on my trip, which is really annoying! It's not cheap and I don't tip, hoping they will learn to give better service. I did also point out this error. Not tipping seems to be fairly common and could be why there are some service issues.

21:30 – Back to the hotel and to bed. Wakeup call is booked for 06:30 as I have a city tour with a harbour lunch cruise and Opera House tour at 08:00.

26/2/06

06:30 – Get up, having not slept much, and make it out of the hotel about 07:00. Tour operator generously agrees to pay my taxi as I'm slightly off route for free hotel pick-ups. I'm more than happy with this.

08:45 – A very late tour but at least it happens. It's ok but no real get-out-and-explore stops, apart from a few five-minute photo stops and thirty minutes in Bondi Beach. It does remind me of some key places from last time when I was just too tired to make the most of my time in Sydney due to bad jet lag!

12 noon – I meet up with a rep from the lunch cruise. He's very bossy, but I don't mind him. I get a table to myself, which I'm actually pleased about—sometimes it can be awkward at a communal table. I enjoy a good buffet lunch. Much like at Ayers Rock, there are oysters, fresh prawns in shells, octopus, etc. Like last night, the mains are a bit blander. I enjoy the harbour tour and this finishes about 14:00.

14:30 – Go on Opera House tour, which is very interesting. It's sad as well, as the original architect fell out with the government and has never visited his creation. He has now mended those bridges, but at eighty-seven years old, if he doesn't fly over soon from Scandinavia, he never will! The concert hall is my favourite part—a massive venue and very attractive.

16:30 – Take the ferry from Circular Quay to the aquarium, which is good fun, a good way to get to it. It's a busy ferry port with loads of small passenger ferries running all the time and they are fast and efficient. The aquarium is busy, as it's Sunday; however my schedule is tight, so this is my only opportunity to go. Impressively, it's open until 22:00 seven days a week. This is good for revenue and is also good for the tourists. My favourite thing is the sharks! It has some huge sharks!

18:50 – I have dinner again at Circular Quay but a different place this time. For starter, I have roast emu, and this is nice and interesting—Rod Hull would be turning in his grave with me eating his poor companion! It is an interesting taste, a cross between venison and beef (served cold). For my main, I have a fairly disappointing seafood risotto, and again this arrives while I'm still eating my starter—this appears to be common practice! I also ask for a bottle of sparkling wine, which is he cheapest wine on the list; two staff members question me whether I'm sure I want a whole bottle to myself and not just a glass of wine! I reply "A bottle please." Am brought just a glass. They remind me, "A bottle is big, you know. Are you sure you won't just accept having a glass of wine…?" "A bottle please!" This goes on for a bit; eventually I get the bottle.

The bill arrives about two-thirds of the way through my main course without me even asking for it. No dessert then, I guess! There is a bad thunderstorm and, while the courtyard area is well sheltered, I think they want to close early, so I just settle my bill. It's not a cheap meal, and the toilets are poor, as again was the service, but the starter was positively memorable, and the sparkling wine was great!

Thunderstorm starts to downpour just as I get back to my hotel, which is good timing!

The friendly receptionist asks me about my day trip. I tell them it was good, and we talk about some ideas for my last day in Sydney as I'm off to the Blue

Mountains tomorrow and Melbourne on Tuesday. Anyway, I'm very tired so off to bed again!

27/2/06
Fairly early start and ready for a day trip to the Blue Mountains. My pick-up arrives in good time, and he's a Glaswegian chap. He is only taking me a short way to the central point and is not my guide for the day. He really likes living in Sydney and wouldn't want to move back to Glasgow. He has lived here about ten years.

I meet up with the guide and a fairly small group of about seventeen of us. Guide is ok; he grows on me as the day goes on. He's a bit of a diva and has a bit of a tantrum when a group of about six Irish people talk quietly while he does his commentary!

It only takes about an hour or so to get to the Blue Mountain area. I think it was the Snowy Mountains Mum and Dad went to, which is much further away. The first thing noticeable on getting out of the bus is it is much, much cooler—probably under fifteen degrees. It's very pretty. We see a few viewpoint areas before having some lunch. Lunch is included in my tour, just a small main course and a drink. I have a frittata, which is very tasty. We are at a nice wee place and I also opt for a lovely homemade lemonade. The other people in my group don't like their meal, but I'm more than happy!

After lunch, we pass through a few pretty villages. We then stop at a rainforest-type place. I think it's called Skyland or something? It's good but very touristy and commercialised. The views are amazing and there are walks and cable-car trips. Also, the world's steepest railway, which is more like a funfair ride than anything! I also see a very faint Aboriginal drawing on a rock.

We are then meant to see some semi-wild kangaroos, but due to bad floods, our bus can't get us there, which is disappointing as I never saw any on my last Australian trip either. Apparently the roos here are quite friendly and may go right up to you. Mum would like that—not! If they don't approach you, don't approach them. I saw a kangaroo bruise covering the whole of a lady's face at the Skyland place—she had tried to pet the roo, but it had other ideas. They are quite funny when angry as they start sparring like a boxer!

We then head back to Sydney. First, we see the Olympic 2000 stadiums, which are amazing. The main stadium was 130,000 capacity but has since been reduced to around 80,000.

To get back to the city centre, our trip includes a leisurely afternoon cruise! This in fact turns out to be a busy, scheduled, fast catamaran ferry. It's good fun though!

On arrival back at Circular Quay, I decide to head back to the hotel and have a cheaper meal at the Italian place next to my hotel—it's in the food court at the shopping centre. It turns out to be pretty good. I start with octopus salad, very nice, and for main I have an ok lasagne—nowhere near as good as Mum's though! I also manage dessert, a two-scoop ice cream. I tip the waitress. In fact, I think this is the first tip I have left since getting to Sydney. She is pleasantly surprised. This good-value place really looked after me.

Off for an early night, as I have another early start with a trip to Melbourne tomorrow!

28/2/06

Get up and ready for a trip to Melbourne. I'm a bit worried about how long it will take to get to the airport, although I know it's only three train stops away. I leave the hotel at 07:15 and catch a train straight away. I get to the airport at 07:55, and within about only five minutes, I've electronically checked in for both my flights out and back and have my boarding pass printed. I have an hour and a half to kill, and enjoy a wander, then some breakfast. Before I know it, it's time to board the short flight to Melbourne. It's pretty much the same flight time as Edinburgh-London, although regionally, Qantas are not as generous with food/drink as the British Airways shuttle were back in the day. You do get a free alcoholic drink on Qantas after 5 p.m.

I get the airport bus into the city and get into the city centre just before 12 noon. I have until 7 p.m., so will have a good day trip ahead of me. I couldn't come to Australia a second time and not make it to Melbourne.

First impressions are not great as the bus/train interchange is basically a building site! They only have two weeks to sort it out in time for the Commonwealth Games—it doesn't look like they will meet this deadline!

A few blocks away and things are much better. There are user-friendly tourist attraction signs, and I spot one for some tower block, top-of-tower viewpoint. This is a good starting point as they play a useful visitor film showing things to do. The view from the top is very impressive.

After this, I intend to go to the aquarium, but after seeing a sign for the immigration museum, I go there instead. Not the best first impressions as the staff carry on with their own conversation when I arrive, despite seeing me. Eventually one of them barks, "What do you want?" I reply, "A ticket please." She then yells, "Where are you from?" I think this is to compile statistics about the visitors.

This is actually an excellent museum and was only a few dollars to buy my ticket. It shows the history of the immigrant and the British influence and the issues with racism. In more recent times, Australia has taken in some vulnerable people from countries such as Vietnam, following the 1977 war, and China, after the Tiananmen Square Massacre, and Ethiopia, after the famine. The other thing that I really enjoy is lots of exhibits/memorabilia about how people got here and the conditions on board many of the ships that arrived full of people until the late 1970s, although in places like the UK these ships generally stopped in the 1960s. This museum has reinforced that it's not impossible for someone with an office-only employment background like me to manage to migrate to Australia! I'm not going to consider this just now, although I really do like Australia!

The next thing I do is get on board a stunning vintage tram on a city loop. Most of the Melbourne trams are now modern; however, for the city loop and a few tram restaurants, they have a few historic trams. Furthermore, the city loop is totally free of charge and the route is almost three miles, lasting about forty minutes, and it generally takes you to all the touristy places! I do a full loop first, which is good fun and gives me a few photo opportunities!

The next stop is the aquarium. I prefer this to the bigger Sydney one. It's nice and quiet, I think due to it being a weekday. There's lots to see, including a dead giant squid preserved in a huge ice cube. It must be about twelve to fifteen feet high and is quite a sight! I always like the seahorses/sea dragons, although I've seen these at many other aquariums before.

It's about 17:15 and I decide to have an early dinner. I find a nice but not cheap restaurant with good views of the river and the park. I watch some rowers, and this part of the river is actually where the Commonwealth Games rowing races will be! It's a fairly cool evening but still pleasant.

I'm at a fairly contemporary Australian restaurant. None of the starters really excite me, and I choose the fairly reliable breaded camembert cheese. For main I choose a kangaroo steak (nice and rare) with a tasty berry sauce. I really enjoy this, and it's a good-sized portion. This is a great meal and a nice setting—it's good just to watch the world go by for a bit. Some interesting wildlife too, such as a yellow and black ladybird, and some very tame birds. During the Australian part of my trip, I must see about fifty different kinds of birds, although not as many parrots as my last time in Australia.

I'm quite late arriving back at the hotel. Flight was about thirty minutes late landing. Most of my flights have been late this trip, although they are with a decent airline. I am delayed further with my airport-to-city train being stuck in a tunnel for about twenty minutes. This is fine, as I have a nice chat with a friendly local Aussie and a Bulgarian lady who, despite only living in Australia for about five years, now has an Australian accent, and in my view could pass for a local! As I'm late in, I decide just to go to bed right away.

1/3/06

March brings the start of autumn to Sydney and it's warm, but there are some brown and red leaves falling off the trees. I enjoy a long lie-in until about 09:30; this is welcome, as I've done so much and need to have a much quieter day.

I'm a bit sad, as this is my last day in Australia, a country I'm very fond of. I have a fantastic breakfast in the little Italian café next to the hotel that I previously mentioned. I enjoy pancakes with maple syrup and cream, freshly squeezed orange juice and a coffee. This does the job and I'm pretty much ready for the day ahead.

Next, I go for a swim and Jacuzzi at my hotel pool. It's a nice cool temperature that possibly puts other people off, so I actually have the pool to myself. It's really steep to get in and out of the pool, but I just about manage—the problem is the tiny foot holes! After another shower in my hotel room, I get the train to Circular Quay and grab a beer in one of the waterside cafés. They are not cheap, even in comparison to the UK, but before my holiday I made the decision that this holiday is entirely about enjoying myself, and if some things are expensive, so be it! All things said, I've not really done anything over the top yet, but very soon you will hear about a special dinner!

Next up, I take the ferry to the zoo. This is one of the older, more interesting ferries and it's just a short fifteen-minute journey. It's a spectacular cable-car trip to the top of the hill where the zoo experience starts. On arrival, I buy a booklet and get my photo taken with some sleeping koalas—these are lovely animals. You are not allowed to touch them though. This zoo is interesting and really good. It's quite a traditional zoo and different to the Singapore one.

I get back to the hotel about 16:30 after spending close to three hours enjoying the zoo.

Just a few doors from the hotel entrance, I hear a familiar voice yelling both "Mikey Needham!" and "Dumbarton!" This is Keith, another of my old team members who married an Australian lady last year, and whom—if you recall—I had tried to get in touch with! Keith is a nice fellow; we got on well when working together. He always told me I was the best boss he ever had, even mentioning this again when we randomly bumped into each other. Flatteringly, he even praised me on Facebook many years later about enjoying being in my team and liking my management style! I went to both Keith's work leaving night, then also his move-to-Australia night.

Sydney has a population of about four million, so bumping into Keith is quite incredible! The fact Michelle thought she'd given me his email address (I tried it, but it rejected) added to the coincidence! Unfortunately, Keith is working until 23:00 and I need to get up at 5 a.m., so it would be crazy to meet up with him later. He only has five minutes to spare, but it's amazing to bump into a friend halfway around the world! Now I have his correct email address, I will send him a note.

The other weird thing today is that I met a second Scottish couple at the zoo. They were a friendly couple and approached me after seeing my Dumbarton top, with our whisky sponsor on it, and noticing my Scottish accent when I participated in a zoo demonstration. They told me they were from Kirriemuir, which was where the only other Scottish couple I spoke to were also from. Turns out it's a little village in the Angus region of Scotland. I mention the other couple to them, but they don't know them.

Anyway, back at the hotel, I enjoy another swim, then my third shower of the day! After this, I hail a taxi as I'm off to arguably the best restaurant in Sydney. It's called 360 Degrees and, in case you didn't guess from that, it's the gourmet revolving restaurant on top of the Sydney Tower. I had checked this place out before my trip and, for what it is, it's good value. My three-course meal, including a bottle of Aussie sparkling wine, is the equivalent of about £55. This may seem a lot, but the food quality combined with location and views is totally exceptional. This is the treat I mentioned earlier.

It starts badly with a stunning female maître d' who decides to deal with two bookings at once. I find this quite rude as I am dumped at my table while the couple are much better treated and welcomed.

To be honest, I'm lucky that they readily accepted my booking for one as, despite it being a Tuesday night, they are totally full. I booked a few nights ago.

I'm assigned two waiters who work well together despite having very different personalities. There's a jokey laid-back chap who claims to have Scottish connections, and a more serious guy.

For my starter, I have a pork belly thing with peeled prawns. It's excellent. For main, I have milk-fed veal with a load of other stuff. I tell Mr Serious it was vealy good. I repeat vealy, *vealy* good—he never gets the joke but tells me he's pleased I enjoyed it and shakes my hand, thanking me for complimenting the food!

Dessert is a wonderful cheeseboard. It is at this stage the service goes downhill, as I observe they have a VIP customer close to me who is totally being fussed over while I am now being ignored. Some tables that have not long arrived actually walk out. I ask three times for butter with my cheese and it takes about forty minutes to finally get this, but eventually I get three different dishes of butter rather than the one dish! To their frustration, I don't touch the cheese until I get the butter, as I'm not in a hurry and enjoying the amazing rotating city views.

After the cheese, I ask for filter coffee. I observe my cup of coffee being offered to practically every other table in the place—eventually I flag to them it's mine!

However, I am quite happy to have stretched my dinner to about three hours. The last funny story from my experience is Mr Serious giving me the bill. As it's a revolving restaurant, the exit nearly arrived at my table. I crack a joke that the exit has arrived to me in perfect timing. He does not get it, so I try to get him to understand. His response is, "I think you're getting confused, sir!"

I get back to the hotel just before 23:00. I'm all packed and ready for a 05:00 start tomorrow!

2/3/06
Yet another really early start. I manage to get up ok, shower and head to reception. My shuttle bus arrives ten minutes early, which is a relief as some locals told me they are not that reliable. Even if it had gone wrong, I'm right by Central Station, which I had previously used for my Melbourne flight. I get to Sydney Airport nice and early and have about two hours to kill.

It's an ok airport. There are ten minutes' free internet. My flight is with Jetstar, which is another Australian airline, quite like EasyJet, and they have links to Qantas, hence this being a QF (Qantas' airline code) codeshare flight. They are ok, but as per my general flight experience, we are about thirty minutes late leaving and arriving in Christchurch.

It's great looking out the plane window, as there are amazing and familiar mountains everywhere and, in contrast, some very flat terrain. I recognise the mountains from *The Lord of The Rings*, as it was filmed nearby. Christchurch is a lovely, pretty city and a nice size, quite a bit smaller than Edinburgh. Very ye olde England, as per Carole's pre-holiday description! After graduating, she did a round-the-world trip, but over about a year rather than just a few weeks!

I check into my Christchurch hotel, which is a four-star, but in my view feels more like a five-star. It's very quiet, as it's now the low season, and is total luxury.

I settle in my room with an enormous bed (queen-size, which is actually bigger than king-size). Unfortunately, I'm only here one night, but I'm glad to get here just after lunch. The lovely cathedral is only a two-minute walk away; I'm actually in Cathedral Square. *(Many years after my trip, both this hotel and the cathedral were completely destroyed in a devastating earthquake.)* My room is on the nineteenth floor with an amazing view. It's well worth the £60 for the night.

I then go on a vintage tram. Due to high winds, most of the tram circuit is closed. My tram is a 1920s one. It's a pretty but little city centre, and such a friendly place. My ticket is a premium one, which was meant to include a cable-car trip; however, due to the high winds the cable car is closed. Without much hassle, I get a part refund for this.

I then go to the aquarium, which is very local and only has New Zealand native wildlife. I am also taken to the kiwi room (not a fruit, but a half-bird/half-mole type creature). I admit I've actually never heard of this creature!

I then visit some lovely shops but don't buy anything. Having seen that the weather in New

York and UK is around freezing, I will soon need to buy a jersey or a jacket! It's quite cool here, about fifteen degrees or slightly less. I've recently been used to double this in Singapore and Australia!

Dinner in the hotel is good, although I just about have the place to myself. I have quail to start, then some quite dear venison (boom boom) and a New Zealand cheeseboard to finish. It's another excellent meal; it's not cheap but it's real quality. The food is paired with really nice local wines.

I enjoy a nice local beer before heading to my room for the night.

Off to bed as flying to Auckland tomorrow; it's just about an hour's flight.

While I remember, I've not actually missed a Dumbarton Football Club match while I've been away. The Alloa game was called off due to the pitch being like a mud bath. The Partick and Gretna games were off, due to both these teams having exceptional cup runs. Both are second-division sides and are at least in the Scottish Cup quarter finals. If Gretna are still in the cup after my trip, I will go and see them (*they, in fact, made the Scottish Cup final. True to my word, I watched both the semi-final win v Dundee and the cruel cup final penalty defeat against Hearts*).

3/3/06

07:00 – A fairly civilised start but unfortunately no time for breakfast. I'm waiting on my airport shuttle bus at 08:00. I'm a bit anxious as I had asked the hotel to book it, advising them that my flight is 09:45, and they suggested booking it for 9 a.m. as it will only take 30 minutes! Thankfully, this is only ten minutes late.

Get to the airport, which for domestic departures

is tiny and does not really have any facilities. I have about an hour to kill after checking in and passing through security.

11:30 – Arrive in Auckland in good time. It's a fairly big city with a population of about 1.25 million. Christchurch is only about 0.25 million.

I find a hotel minibus. Get to Aspin House Hotel, which has very big rooms. Again, it's excellent value at £40 a night. Settle in and decide to sleep for a bit as could do with a rest. I head into the city centre, which is only a short walk away. It's a hustle-and-bustle kind of place, but I soon understand things more after getting my bearings. I eventually find the "hop-on hop-off" bus. It's a fairly bland pre-recorded commentary, but in the main, it's a good way of getting to grips with a new city. It only takes about thirty minutes or thereabout to do the circuit, which is one of the shortest city tours I've been on.

After the bus, I find a tourist information office. I go there to try to get on a winery tour. I had made a few calls earlier, but because I was on my own and it's the low season, I had been unable to secure a guided winery trip and, with no transport, it didn't seem easy to do a self-planned trip.

The good news is the tourism office sorts everything out. The lady is helpful to me but quite rude to her colleague, who is new and has an "in training" badge on her jersey. The lady helping me yells to her, "In-training, do this," as she can't remember her name! Like I say, she's helpful to me though, and persuades a tour operator to do a winery tour of Waiheke island, which is about a forty-minute ferry trip away. This is all booked for tomorrow.

I then find a nice pub by the waterside. It's not cheap, but I sit outside and enjoy a nice beer.

I then go for dinner, bypassing some really expensive places until I find a really nice but more affordable seafood place. I start with half-a-dozen Oysters Mornay, then for main I give in to temptation and choose the seafood platter! This is massive and contains green-tipped mussels, cold oysters, calamari in batter, prawns in batter and a small cod. This is superb and goes so well with a chilled bottle of local sauvignon blanc wine! Being greedy, I decide I can manage dessert and, in predictable manner, opt for the cheeseboard. It's only two different cheeses, but both are really nice. Cheese in Australia and New Zealand is much nicer than in UK hotels. Service is good, so they earn a decent tip.

Back to hotel for a very early night—it's not even 20:00!

4/3/06

08:00 – Another more civilized start to the day. My ferry to Waiheke Island is not until 10 a.m., so I can enjoy a leisurely start to the day. A basic breakfast is included, so I grab a coffee and some fruit. I leave the hotel at about 09:15 as it's only a short walk. It's 09:30 and I go to a nice coffee shop opposite the pier; I grab a cappuccino. Not much of a queue, but the very casual staff are really slow. It takes too long to get served, and then another ten minutes to actually get the coffee to my table. I practically down it in one so I'm not rushing for the ferry!

I manage to catch the ferry ok. It's pretty busy, as it's Saturday. I had actually lost track of the days until today!

Arriving at the island, I get a friendly welcome from the tour guide. There is also a nice middle-aged lady on my tour. We go to three wineries, all very pleasant in different ways and all are in stunning locations. Between the three vineyards, I sample eleven different wines and two oils—one olive and one avocado. The samples are quite small so there is no getting drunk. I end up buying a lovely Riesling and the nicest olive oil I have tasted! I love this island soooo much!

I'm a bit disappointed that I can't have lunch at a vineyard; the problem is they are too far from the ferry and our guide is unavailable from now. He has, however, been really good, and we got a mini island tour.

I'm dropped off at a nice wee restaurant near the ferry. The food is good but the service not so— the waitress can't, and doesn't really attempt to, understand me. I ask for a glass of local wine. When she eventually understands me, she answers that she doesn't know what's local or not, no effort to find out. I think I choose a local one—it's really nice anyway! I order a really nice homemade burger. A long time after I'm finished, my plate is finally cleared and I'm asked if I want dessert. I seem to reply in a foreign language as I keep saying "Yes, please," and she keeps saying "Sorry?" Eventually she appears to understand yes! After twenty minutes, still no dessert menu. I attract a different waitress and she seems more attentive. I order excellent homemade ice cream and choose white chocolate, banana and strawberry yogurt, which are amazing. I then order a coffee and cancel it, as it still hasn't arrived after fifteen minutes. I'm the only customer in the place and the ferry is due to leave in about fifteen minutes. It's only a few minutes' walk, but I don't want to down another coffee. Takes ages to pay the bill, and now I'm in a hurry.

Halfway to the ferry, I realise that I've left the

wine and olive oil. No way I'm leaving that, and the ferry is every half hour, so it's not a huge deal, but I now accept I need to get the next one. I will now have a nice beer. The reason I sort of rushed myself is my "hop-on hop-off" bus is valid until the end of today, but the last bus is 4 p.m. There is an Antarctic museum in the city outskirts, which would be quite a walk. Beer and weather have both been nice, and despite my experience, I did enjoy the restaurant.

I catch the next ferry and head back to the hotel. I laze about for a bit, then off to dinner. I come across a nice gastropub with a nautical theme—I think it was called Mack's? They have a beer menu as well as a food one. As I'm not hungry, I decide just to have a main course and choose the pig's belly, which is fantastic! The beer is great too, with friendly service!

After my meal, I find a postbox and send the last of my postcards. I then go into another nice pub and have a second pint but decide that's enough after all my wine-tasting.

Back to the hotel and off to bed.

5/3/06
Groundhog Day!

Tomorrow will also be today as I gain an extra day. I arrive in Los Angeles about five hours before I leave Auckland, how cool/weird is that!

Anyway, I leave the luggage and head off to the ferry port. I'm off to another aquarium. This one is a bit different as it has Antarctic memorabilia and also a penguin sanctuary! There is meant to be a taxi boat to take you to the aquarium, but apparently it's not running. I grab an ice cream and decide to walk as it's a nice day. It's about a three-and-a-half mile walk and takes me about an hour and a half. I'm glad to get there! It's busy due to being a Sunday, but it's a good attraction. It's quite small though and, even taking my time, only takes about an hour to go around. The penguins are really interesting and funny. They are all individual characters with different personalities. I also love the seahorses, as per any aquarium!

I decide to get the bus back. While waiting, I freak myself out by noticing I'm covered in spots on my hands and arms. I think it's a heat rash, as I am feeling totally fine.

I still have a couple of hours to kill and decide to have a late lunch at the pub where I had dinner last night and enjoy a nice minute steak sandwich.

I get back to the hotel and catch my airport connection.

At the airport, I face the reality of another really long flight with zero leg room! I cheekily decide to ask for an upgrade, which is declined. I ask for an aisle seat and am ignored and end up being given a middle seat. I'm annoyed as I've checked in really early. After complaining at the departure gate, I get my aisle seat. Why didn't the other lady just give me this?!

The flight is actually really good and, before I know it, we're in Los Angeles. When asked by the friendly girl sat next to me if I'm here for the Oscars, I tell her I'm up for an Oscar as I'm Nick Park, the famous creator of Wallace and Gromit. This was good fun to do, and I was just having a bit of harmless fun. This was in the days before social media, so no embarrassing picture with a Walter Mitty impersonator!

Arrive in LA after about a fourteen-hour flight! Still 5/3/06.

This is my first time in America and first impressions are that the security employees are horrible, rude and abrupt! I am sent back to the end of the queue after missing out a small section of the form, which it's not at all obvious you should complete! I'm furious at the robotic jobsworth. Second guy is not much better; he yells at me for not easily managing to use the fingerprint scanner! I tell him to slow down and calm down, but in hindsight I maybe could have got myself into some bother! I think I'd better grin and bear it if I come across more rude security people. Post-9/11, security is understandably tight in America.

I have not booked a transfer but manage to get a walk-on hotel minibus quickly. I think I'm quite lucky, as it's busy and the buses are all pretty full. I get to the hotel, which, as described, is grand and 1930s art deco. The receptionists are stunning Hispanic ladies who are chatting in Spanish; they are possibly from Mexico, which is quite close by. My room won't be ready for about three hours. I then politely show my paperwork, which indicates I'm only one hour early, not three hours! I don't sleep on flights, so really need my bed. I insist on getting my room in around an hour!

I ask where I can get some lunch and end up at a nice and popular pizza place. It's very busy but I manage to get a table. I have a lovely bacon and avocado pizza and a homemade lemonade to drink. It's good and, as per the guidebooks, I tip fifteen percent—a good value lunch.

Back to the hotel, I am pleased with my room. I have something I've not had before, which is a proper coffee machine, so no instant coffee! I go for a sleep.

After five or so hours, I get up and have a shower.

It's an awful shower! I like the hotel though—
it reminds me of the old Glasgow Central Hotel
before it was refurbished, a bit old-world scruffy,
but in a charming, past-grandeur sort of way!

I phone to book my table for tomorrow. I'm so
excited because I'm off to dine on Queen Mary at
Long Beach. This is a retired ocean liner, which is
very original and is now a hotel ship!

I have dinner at my hotel as I don't want to
venture too far tonight. I have a steak, which is ok
but a bit gristly. The waiters are real characters
in their demeanour. Overall, I enjoy it. I just have
the one course, then go back to my hotel room to
watch the Oscars! Many people will be jealous of
me being in LA on Oscar night, which was a total
coincidence. I'm quite lucky to have got a decent
deal on my hotel! This was partly why I didn't head
to the city centre, as it would be really busy—might
have seen some celebs though! I enjoy watching it
on my bedroom's TV. I've hardly watched any TV
during my trip. Tomorrow, I will see many of the
places I'm watching on TV just now!

After a good sleep, I wake up wondering if
Groundhog Day is over? Incidentally, this is one of
my favourite films!

Yes, it's now *6/3/06*.

Have an ok breakfast at the hotel, although it
reminds me of McDonalds breakfasts! Then head
off to find my LA stars walking tour. They were not
very helpful when I called to reconfirm this trip.
The hotel concierge also didn't help me, as all they
were interested in was selling me all sorts of trips
that I politely declined!

Firstly, on leaving my hotel, I struggle to find
the Metro (underground) train. Eventually, I see a
tiny sign. Not many people use the Metro as most

people have cars. I end up in the wrong place, actually arriving at the PO Box of the tour company. When I find the actual correct start point, it turns out I had passed it earlier!

I'm about an hour late, but the friendly Geordie tour guide is fine about it and books me into the next tour in about an hour and a half's time. He talks about his past as a Beefeater in the Tower of London and says that he loves living in LA. He actually got married on the Queen Mary and is impressed I'm going there for dinner tonight!

The tour is really good with excellent explanations about the speakeasies (as per American Prohibition in the 20s—no alcohol)! I would not have coped! Also, I get interesting stories and explanations about the first premier cinema, the first red carpet cinema, the Hollywood sign, the Oscars and the stars on the pavement. We're unlucky with the weather as it pours with rain for about an hour— not meant to do this in Hollywood!

After the tour, I go back to the hotel, shower and change for my special meal—dinner on the Queen Mary. It retired from its scheduled transatlantic service to be replaced by the QE2 in the early 1970s. I have looked forward to this since I booked my round-the-world trip!

I give myself over two and a half hours to get there, as I understand (partly from Carole's advice) that it's a long journey away. The Metro map shows I need to go on two end-to-end lines! It turns out to be a bit of a nightmare to get to as I didn't realise I need a bus after the Metro. I manage to get on two wrong buses and arrive about thirty minutes late! The reassuring and kind lady tells me not to worry, and they are not too busy anyway, partly with it being midweek.

I have a massive meal including lobster bisque and Steak Wellington. It's very traditional; you can imagine being on here eating these things back in the 1930s and '40s! It's one of my favourite meals ever and, after finishing my meal, the lovely staff totally encourage me to explore the ship. I have a brief wander as I'm a bit worried about the journey home, although it should be a bit easier than getting here was!

Getting back to the hotel takes about two hours without any mistakes. While this was a long way, it was so worth it—just amazing! Head to bed immediately on getting back to the hotel, as it's an early start tomorrow to pick up my flight to New York!

7/3/06

Early start but manage to get up ok. Transport is fifteen minutes late, always a slight panic with booked airport pick-ups, but to date I've not had any that went totally wrong! A battered A-Team-type black van arrives. I thought there was a Scottish twang in the driver's accent, but he tells me he's Polish. I'm the only person in the van and the road is pretty quiet. Takes under an hour, and I spot John Travolta's own private, ex-Qantas Boeing 707. He is a qualified pilot and likes to fly himself to places. It's a seriously cool retro aircraft!

Check-in is fairly smooth. American Airlines are ok; they are no longer a full-fat airline, especially for domestic flights. There are some things included, such as soft drinks, but no free food. I had researched this before my trip started. The lady next to me is annoying. She wants to get up lots of times during the five-hour flight, but I'm sometimes too slow in reacting and she climbs over me twice!

I assume she's unwell and accept this situation, avoiding a conflict! It's an ok day flight.

I'm tired on arrival into New York. New York is cold and looks frosty, although I believe the roads are just a whiter colour and don't think it's actually frost.

The transfer takes ages, but I like the driver and we have a good chat about things we have in common, such as food and travel appreciation.

Am pleased to get to the hotel, which is in the trendy area of Tribeca within Manhattan. Don't get a very friendly welcome from the receptionist!

First thing I do is shower, as I stink! Travelling seems to cause this! I then, with guidance from my guidebook, book dinner for tomorrow night. I book the French Institute of Catering (*sadly this gem is no longer open; it was a training restaurant for budding chefs who wanted to work at the very highest standard*).

I then take a wander around the corner of the hotel, spotting a pub/burger/Mexican-type eatery! I start with chilli nachos followed by a blue cheese burger. The meal is fine, washed down with Budweiser beer on tap. I enjoy this cheap meal, no room for dessert. I like the waitress; she's not busy and really only has me to look after, so is generally reading her book. She pretty much says "uh huh" to everything I say!

I head off to bed but really struggle to sleep as it's so noisy, if not quite Egypt levels. It's exciting to be here though!

8/3/06

I have a bit of a lie-in, mainly due to being tired. I grab a Starbucks coffee from next to my hotel. My hotel doesn't have any catering service, but that's not an issue as it's a really good location for coffees and meals. I try to grab the subway but, as in LA, it's not straightforward. First, I don't understand how to buy the day ticket. The auto machine is unclear and the guy at the ticket booth is so unhelpful; he won't sell me a day ticket and refers me back to the machine—what does he sell then?! I end up buying a single ticket.

The subway is too complex. For example, my stop, Chambers Street, as per many stops, is not just one station, as Chambers Street runs through about four blocks. There are several Chambers Street stations, but you need to be on the right one, e.g. the red or blue line! I'm going to Times Square and thankfully there is just one Times Square stop!

On arriving at Times Square, I find a sweater shop and get a cheap jersey for about $10. It's not as cold as I thought it might be. I'm lucky as there was really heavy snow only two days before I got here! I eventually manage to find the tour bus office where I exchange my pre-booked voucher for a ticket and guidebook. All goes to plan, apart from operating hours. Was advertised in the UK as running every ten minutes until 22:00, but in reality it runs every thirty minutes until 18:00. While this is a pain, I would have still booked this anyway!

Tour is very good. I like the live commentary, so much better than the pre-recorded ones you often get! I get off at the ferry taking me to the Statue of Liberty. I already have a pre-booked ticket for this. I need to go through an X-ray security machine with heightened security following 9/11. It doesn't take long. The ferry is very busy, but Liberty Island is interesting. You can't go up the statue itself unless you book in advance—I never even knew this was an option anyway. It's very nice and such a world-famous landmark.

I get back to Manhattan and catch an underground train back to my hotel. I then change and tidy myself up for another special dinner in the French Institute place. The food is amazing on a table d'hote menu. My waitress is an English actress; she is charismatic, and I do like her. This is another fantastic meal of the highest quality!

I head back to the hotel after another busy day.

9/3/06

Get up a bit earlier today and find an amazing Vienna-type café very close to the hotel. It's outstanding and I enjoy pancakes with maple syrup and fruit, freshly squeezed orange juice and lovely coffee.

I then find the tour bus again as I have a forty-eight-hour "hop-on hop-off" ticket.

I try to go to the Maritime Museum, but it's shut. No obvious reason why, which is a shame as it has a lot of stuff that was on the ill-fated Titanic ship! Back on the bus and get off at the Rockefeller Centre, which is a massive tower. It isn't too busy and has amazing views from the top. Its design, with see-through plastics and glass, make the view amazing.

Next, I explore some of the other areas in the city, such as Harlem and Brooklyn; these are very interesting!

When the bus takes me back to Times Square I go to TKTS, just like the one on Leicester Square in London's Theatreland! As per London, no real bargains. I settle for going to see *Candyfloss*, which is an American Dream-type show where an ordinary American teenager becomes a famous dancer. It's ok, some catchy songs. Also, this being my first trip to an American theatre, I discover that the show programme is free—the usherettes hand them out! I also have a Cuban meal before the show. It's ok, nothing special. I had previously had a Cuban meal when in Dubai.

10/3/06 – Last day of my trip
As I reflect on some of the adventures I've had, it's been an amazing trip! I have almost a full day in New York before my overnight flight back to London Heathrow.

I get up about 08:30 and head back to the great café by my hotel. I have another pancake breakfast. The most noticeable thing today is that it's nice and warm, about the high teens, and this signals the start of nice spring days!

After breakfast, I go and pay my respects to the memorial at Ground Zero. It's an emotional thing to do, and I'm glad I do this. I say a prayer in my head.

I then take the long underground trip to wander round a small part of the huge and pretty Central Park. It's peaceful and a happy park. It's great to be here in such nice weather.

I then head off to the Empire State Building. The queue takes about an hour. It's a good experience and such a famous landmark. It's not as good a view as the Rockefeller Centre. I think that less queuing and an even a better view made the other one a better experience!

I then head back in the direction of my hotel, and I get my hair cut in a dirt-cheap trainee place. This times me nicely for being back at the hotel in time for my airport transfer. It's late arriving and a rival company tries to tout me, but I do the right thing and wait. Before long, it arrives. The roads are actually so bad and it's a very bumpy ride. I'm just glad I have the common sense to wear my seat belt!

My British Airways flight to Heathrow is about an hour late, and the British Airways part of the JFK Airport terminal is on the small side. I also complain again, as despite checking in really early and asking for my usual aisle seat, I get another middle one. I complain as they are not willing to change me—that is, until I ask to speak to a manager, and suddenly it's no problem to get me an aisle seat!

It's a fantastic flight and I'm addressed as Mr Needham by all the attendants. Very impressive for a 747 Jumbo Jet in economy. After arriving at Heathrow (pre-Terminal 5), transferring to a domestic flight takes ages. I end up with about an hour free, so catch up with emails. Flight is delayed a bit, so I'm hoping this doesn't cause Mum too much of an issue as she is meeting me off the flight.

I'm quite hyper on the flight, reflecting on my amazing trip. I am met by my mum, and this is a great way to end the holiday of a lifetime. I then go for a coffee, sharing some of the stories of my adventures. I hope you've enjoyed me sharing this experience, and I highly recommend doing a trip like this!

CHAPTER 9

Travel Agency Trips

Working in travel was an amazing experience. I was lucky to mainly work for a long-haul tour operator and, while the money wasn't great, it was more than made up for by the travel opportunities (generally known as educational trips) given to me to improve my destination skills and knowledge. Our customers were travel agents, who then in turn sold our flights, hotels, transfers, sightseeing trips, cruises and tours to their customers.

I had sourced my own trip to Thailand, having liaised with a long-haul travel publication that had a last-minute space. I was offered this, but my work knocked back the late request—understandable, as little notice was given. However, I couldn't hide my disappointment. I think the reasons were partly to do with me recently being upskilled to first- and business-class flight sales.

To my employer's credit, they really made an effort to get me on an educational. After the turned-down Thailand trip, within a month or so, my manager called me into a room. She and her boss then offered me a trip to Australia! This would be my third time in Australia. My second trip was covered in the separate chapter on my round-the-world trip and was one of the biggest motivators for me ending up working for a long-haul travel tour operator.

I'm quite lucky to have found the Western Australia itinerary for the first half of the trip, which has helped refresh my memory considerably in writing up an amazing trip!

This trip was to Perth and Sydney. We were to meet at Glasgow Airport and get the shuttle to Gatwick. We were told to dress smartly as there was a chance of an airport lounge in Gatwick, then possibly business-class flights either to Dubai or even to Perth.

10-11 March 2009 (overnight flight)
Everyone was dressed well, but then Allister arrived looking like Crocodile Dundee. He had a leather cowboy hat and ripped jeans. There was panic as he couldn't really access the lounge dressed how he was. I immediately thought on my feet and said that I had a spare pair of chinos, but these were are about double the size he needed!

He accepted my offer and headed to the toilet. Five minutes later, he arrived back with clearly oversized trousers on and looked really silly. He's a heck of a nice guy, one of the friendliest in the office, and would do anything to help you. He had also worked for the company a long time, and this was his first educational opportunity.

We arrived at security and Allister was in front of me. He went through the X-ray machine and *beep…beep…beep*. He was asked back and told to empty his pockets, and, unusually, he presented two screwdrivers! He was asked why?! And his answer was that he was sorting an issue with a colleague's desk, exactly the kind-hearted thing he used to do. He went back through the machine and *bleep… bleep…bleep*. "Take off your belt, please." Oh no!!!

He took the belt off and his trousers fell down in

front of the Glasgow airport security team. Worse, he was commando, with no underwear on, so he was completely exposing his genitals!!!

Some of us, myself included, were practically rolling about the floor as it was so funny, but a bit serious as well! Security were decent about this and Allister was not in any trouble and had now cleared security!

We had a nice BA flight to Gatwick and, on arrival, our lead guide, Shirley, took us to the fantastic airport lounge. Allister thanked me again for helping him out and we had a laugh about his mistakes and the adventure so far. He offered to get me a G&T, thanking me for my help in getting him into the lounge, and came back with a gin with a splash of tonic—strongest I've ever had! I drank this for a good hour and declined his offers for a top-up. I also managed a small glass of champagne—Veuve Cliquot no less, love this one, probably more than Bollinger or Möet! We also met the rest of the group. There were travel agents from different parts of the UK and a guide from Germany.

We then went to board our flight and were told the good news that we would be upgraded all the way to Australia. We had one change of aircraft about a third of the way there. Allister was quite drunk and was moved next to one of the more senior members of the group for the final flight. The cabin crew were not happy with him during the final flight and he actually ended up being sent back home. He resigned from the job on the flight back. Hard not to feel sorry for him, getting this opportunity and getting all the way to Australia, then it all going so wrong.

The group agreed to put this behind us and enjoy our trip. We were greeted by our coach driver, who randomly had the same name as an ex prime minister! He took us to our Perth hotel for the first night. We checked into our modern, stylish city hotel and enjoyed a casual dinner. On travel agent trips, you generally share a room, so we learned who we were paired up with. I shared with Duncan, a nice cheerful fellow, quite quiet, but I guess I am as well.

It was so good to get to bed after the dinner. I was truly knackered—there was no going for a drink or anything like that, or certainly not for me!

Friday 12 March 2009
After breakfast, we had a bit of a city tour on the coach before heading to the botanical gardens to go on a new feature, which was not there the last time I was in Perth—a high-up walkway with good views of the city and gardens.

We then went on to Fremantle and headed to the amazing Esplanade hotel. I just love the frontier look of this hotel, and inside it really impressed me too! I enjoyed a quick tour around the hotel, looking at the various room types, and decided that if I come back to the Perth area, I would stay here—and the lead-in room type is more than fine for me!

We then headed to a lovely seaside town called Busselton and had lunch at a really nice restaurant called The Goose, which had lovely views of the coast.

After lunch, we went for a walk on the old pier. At about two kilometres in length, it's not just the longest pier in Australia but the whole of the Southern Hemisphere! It was a nice walk, but it was hard not to notice that it's very tired and worn and in need of extensive renovation, which—I'm pleased to say—a Google search has confirmed has since been done! There was also an underground observatory, and we were able to see colourful fish by some coral.

Busselton broke our journey up nicely, and next stop was the famous wine town of Margaret River. The wines here were amazing. I especially liked some of the white wines here, such as the sauvignon blanc. We checked into our apartment-type hotel rooms and I went for a swim in the outdoor pool to relax for a short while, before meeting at reception for a chat with the general manager over a glass of wine. The GM was very knowledgeable and made good recommendations when we were choosing a glass of wine.

We then headed to the aptly named Wino's for our dinner! We mingled with locals there—it's a very informal pub type place—and enjoyed a nice meal and especially enjoyed some good wines too!

We somehow found our lodge-type apartments. I would probably have struggled if I'd been on my own, as their number system wasn't easy to follow!

For breakfast, we headed to a really trendy café—The Dome Café—and enjoyed a nice breakfast with particularly good coffees.

Then it was time for a cool adventure. We met our friendly guide, who was quite a character! He brought out a live witchetty grub—the thick, white, huge, ugly caterpillar, well known as a dodgy food trial on the popular jungle entertainment show, *I'm a Celebrity, Get Me Out of Here!* The guide asked if anyone was brave enough to try the grub. Without any hesitation, I said yes please! Before handing me it, he told me I was the first in months to accept the challenge! You know, I actually enjoyed it and thought it tasted strongly of tomato! Google describes the typical taste as more like prawn or chicken, but my one was definitely closer to a tomato flavour! Grant, whom I worked with, manned up to the challenge and also had one. He didn't mind it either! The funny guide then offered us snakes to eat. They turned out to be jelly snakes—was a bit disappointed!

Then we got our canoes. I had been a bit nervous about these before the trip. I was worried they would be the individual ones with the short hole, as I was really worried about capsizing and getting out of it easily, but they carried about four people. I had flagged a few concerns when the itinerary arrived, but one of the organisers rightly said that I should have flagged these concerns before the itinerary arrived. At this time, I didn't know that I was dyspraxic.

We grouped ourselves up and our group was a relaxed one that didn't do anything silly. I actually did really well on the boat; I had good rowing experience from my past times in the boat hire on the River Tweed in Peebles. The group were impressed with my rowing. We rowed for quite a bit, and then stopped in a bit that was well populated by wildlife. The guide pointed out loads of not-too-dangerous creatures to us! He also told us about some Aboriginal tales.

We headed back to the main area and some of the groups were larking about. My friend Shirley shouted that their boat was stuck. We headed over to help them, but there were wasps everywhere, so we abandoned that idea. Somehow, they overturned their boat and got totally soaked! Our group made it back dry, but I think the other two boats got completely drenched! Thankfully, basic showers and the fact our luggage was on the coach meant anyone wet was able to shower and change!

Our next stop was a posh winery, Vasse Felix, the oldest in the area. We enjoyed a delicious lunch and wine tasting in outstanding surroundings; it was a real treat.

Unfortunately, we were behind schedule and had to miss out on the chocolate shop.

Next up was another amazing treat. We were off to Cape Lodge, one of the best restaurants in the world! It's a boutique hotel, vineyard and restaurant. We had a lovely tour, then afternoon tea, which was amazing and very sophisticated! All the girls fancied the GM here, saying he looked like George Clooney!

I declared this to have been one of the best days ever, as we were then on our way to the Bootleg brewery for a tasting paddle of beer each. Each glass was about a quarter-pint of beer, and we enjoyed four lovely, fresh craft beers. No time for another round, sadly, as we only managed about thirty minutes here, but it was nice to sit out in the sunshine. A beer garden is hard to beat when the weather is half decent!

We then arrived late at our hotel for the night, which was another stunning place, right on the sea, the aptly named Seashells Resort Yallingup. We had a nice dinner. Again, we dined outside, enjoying great food at the hotel, fine wine and nice company.

13 March 2009
Enjoyed a nice breakfast inside the very attractive hotel restaurant.

We then headed to a nearby cave—nearby in Australian terms, anyway. It was about forty-five minutes on the coach. I'd never been to a proper cave before and found it quite interesting.

We had lunch at a local hotel, then went on a 4x4 adventure tour through forest and beach. The Great Southern Ocean was spectacular to see.

Our next stop was a real delight—Karri Valley Resort. This was a stunning lodge place. I loved the lodges, which were generally two-bed ones. They all had real log fires, and the smell of lighting these in the early evening was great. The sales manager here was so friendly and we enjoyed her company at dinner. She was such fun; it felt as if I had known her for a long time. It's great to meet characters like her.

After dinner, we went into one of the cabins to relax, chat and enjoy some more wine. It was good to be in such a nice group of mainly like-minded people. I had a laugh with Martina, a German lady. She asked me whether my roommate's name was pronounced "Duncan" or "Dooonkan". I said it's Dooonkan, then she said Dooonkan…. The whole group was in fits of laughter, and both Martina and Duncan saw the funny side too! I can be a bit naughty at times!

I also failed badly in the challenge of starting a real fire and keeping it going. It's practical things like this and DIY that I struggle with—don't think I mentioned the time I was hammering screws into my new Ikea futon! Mum and her partner just about managed to repair the futon for me!

14 March 2009
I did exactly what my itinerary suggested and took an early-morning walk around the lovely lake. If I recall, it took about an hour and a half, but was such a lovely walk.

Had breakfast, and I embarrassingly had to tell the staff that sometimes the psoriasis on my scalp/head could be really bad and could bleed. I apologised for making a mess of the pillow and offered to replace it. They and the group were very sympathetic. It was an unexpected bleed, doesn't happen often.

After checking out, we headed to the Gloucester Tree. This was another activity I was a bit worried about. They said it wasn't mandatory, but those that wanted to could climb the tree. It was a very wide tree used to look out for forest fires. I only managed a few steps, but Grant and Duncan (foolishly wearing flip-flops) both made it to the lookout and back down again. I'm glad I went up a little bit, but it was a really tricky climb and there was no real safety protection, so the climb was at our own risk. There was no way I could have managed this, or I would have risked my life!

We then headed round a woodcraft gallery. Here, I bought some nice turned-wood coasters for presents. There were some lovely pieces of furniture.

We were running late, so had a very quick lunch at the Cidery and had a quick look at the orchards full of autumn colours.

We had a long drive back to Perth, about four hours. On the last few days, we took scenic routes, but going back we were on the highway all the way. We were all really tired and I made the well-received suggestion that we stop for fifteen minutes at a service station for a coffee and a stretch, as four hours in one go is hard going. It was a local wee place we stopped at. It was quite good fun, as we noticed different accents and it wasn't in the least bit a touristy place to stop, but they had ok coffee and toilets, and it was good to stretch the legs!

After the second half of the long highway drive, we got to our next hotel, which was really nice. It was the Esplanade River Suites, and what I really liked about this one was having a Jacuzzi spa bath—all the rooms had these. I made the most of the hour or so of free time and enjoyed the Jacuzzi for a bit.

Then we headed to dinner. We were hosted by a senior member of Tourism Australia and we were at a lovely seafood restaurant. We had a lovely meal, but I was so tired. It was an amazing experience here and I was very sad to be leaving, but equally excited to be heading to Sydney the next day.

15 March 2009
Early start, about 5 a.m., to get to the airport and catch an early morning flight to Sydney.

We checked into our hotel at Darling Harbour, which was an area I didn't know too well. It was nice and near the aquarium. The hotel was also very close to Chinatown.

Good news—my boss Danielle got back after chaperoning Allister back to Glasgow. It was a shame she had missed the Western Australia part, but it was nice to have her back.

We only had an hour or so free before our first activity, a bike tour around Sydney. I was quite nervous about this and my ability—as you may recall from earlier in the book, I'm lucky to have managed to learn how to ride a bike, although it's not my strongest area!

One of the group pulled out on capability grounds, but I came to Australia with the view that I would give everything a try. I enjoyed this activity and there were quite a few miles involved! I found some of the places very interesting and it was a great way to see the city. We went over the Harbour Bridge twice, and it was a good way to cross it.

The tour was a few hours long, then we headed back to the hotel to get tidied up. Dinner that night was a river cruise dinner experience. The food was a good set menu, although having done the lunch cruise, I preferred that one—mainly due to the seafood buffet starter, I think!

When we got back, we were all excited to be in Sydney and wanted to make the most of it before going to bed. The rest of the group wanted to know where was open late. This was my third time in Sydney, so I let them know that City Extra was open twenty-four hours. We enjoyed some wine there, with a nice view over the harbour.

16 March 2009

We were off to the Blue Mountains. We were picked up in a really cool, off-road-type minibus, and the group immediately liked our driver and guide.

On the way, we stopped at a wildlife park, where we were given a bag of food each to hand-feed the kangaroos! We then went to Scenic World—I covered this in my round-the-world trip but may have called it by the wrong name.

We were given a short ride on an old London bus when we got near the hotel. I was really looking forward to the hotel stay, as we were going to Lilianfels, which was an Orient Express hotel, while I was there. This boutique hotel was totally stunning and we had our own rooms, which was a bonus. We had the afternoon free and I enjoyed walking around the grounds and going for a swim in the outdoor pool. Most of the group sunbathed. There were also some nice walks and bike trips, and we were told we could borrow mountain bikes. At dinner, we had such a laugh talking about our experiences so far.

17 March 2009

After a leisurely start to the day, we had an amazing breakfast, then headed back to Sydney. We were staying in the Rocks area. We visited a nice four-star hotel, the Harbour Rocks hotel, which was of a similar standard to the one we were staying in, but it was really quirky. I think I encouraged Mum to book the same one.

We then went to the aquarium, which I had been to before but still really enjoyed. We had an informal, canteen-style lunch there before a whistle-stop walk round, as we were behind schedule.

We then headed to do the Opera House tour—I was happy to be doing this again as it's such an iconic place! Dinner tonight was at a pub I'd also been to before, but last time, I just had a drink; this time pizza. I think my one was crocodile and cactus—really! There is very little I won't eat!

18 March 2009

At breakfast time, we were taken to one of the amazing five-star hotels and went to the club floor for an amazing breakfast. We then went to the Harbour Bridge Climb. Carole had warned me that I might not manage this so well, so I was a bit nervous about it. I told our group that I didn't want to be first or last. Not everyone did this activity, but again, in the spirit of giving everything a try, I didn't pull out. We were all breathalysed, to the same standards as if we were driving, and we all passed this! The climb was a great experience and, while the heights were quite scary, I'm so glad to have done this.

After lunch at a funky hotel in the Coodgie Beach area, we went to meet up with Big Wave Dave and do some surfing at Bondi Beach. Again, I gave this a try and was so bad at it that I was given my own instructor! She was a lovely lady and was patient with me. While I was unable to stand on the board, I did get better at catching the wave at the right time and enjoyed going quite fast towards the beach. Again, this was an activity I would never have chosen to do, but I'm glad to have done it.

We enjoyed the last night of our amazing trip at the luxury hotel. The room was amazing, the view was incredible and I loved the electronic blinds—real cool to press a button to open/close the blinds. Sadly, after this night, we were going back to Glasgow, having had an amazing trip.

* * *

African Adventure
About a year later, I was told that if I could make my own way to Zimbabwe and back from South Africa, I would get to experience a vintage African hotel train adventure.

There were exceptional Emirates business-class deals on around this time, and I chose to make the trip even more special by flying Emirates business-class return. To get the deal to work, I had to fly out from Newcastle but would fly back to Glasgow.

I stayed in the Novotel in Newcastle Airport for one night, which had a swimming pool. I went to a nearby carvery place for dinner.

I liked the older Airbus from Newcastle to Dubai. The business-class seat was more like a comfy armchair than an airline seat. I also had a nice lady sat next to me. The food was like fine dining and the wine was some of the best I've had. The highlight was the luxury cheese trolley—top-class cheese and generous accompanying port to drink!

The huge business-class lounge in Dubai seemed never-ending; there were loads of different seating areas, bars and restaurants and all-included Veuve Clicquot champagne to drink—don't mind if I do!

Stopping in Dubai for three or four hours split the journey nicely. There are quicker options, but for such a good airline and avoiding going via London, this option suited me.

After another great flight to Johannesburg, I found my way to my airport hotel fairly easily through the complimentary hotel bus. Hotel was nice, typical four-star airport hotel, no swimming pool but nice rooms. I checked in around lunchtime and went straight to bed. I was really tired as I don't sleep on planes, never have—even with the lie-flat beds in business class. I managed to sleep for about six hours, then had an ok dinner at the hotel. There was a conflict at the end as the cheeky waiter was angry and suggested I should have tipped more than the fifteen percent I gave him! I was totally unimpressed and headed back to my room. I didn't complain further about this.

I had a nice breakfast the next morning and a different waiter was more attentive, friendly and chatty. However, on checking out of my room, reception took ages—like fifteen minutes—don't know why they were so slow, there wasn't a queue or anything. I asked the minibus to wait, but it didn't. I'd given myself ten minutes, thinking this would be ample time. The bus was very regular, so it was no real hardship and I had given myself a good two and a half hours or so to complete the pre-flight formalities and enjoy the airport. Even with the next transfer, checking in for the Zimbabwe flight was straightforward and I had plenty of time to look though the airport shops. The shops were really nice and quite crafty—all a bit different than at most airports.

I caught my South African Air short flight from Johannesburg (South Africa) to Victoria Falls (Zimbabwe). I was pleased to be in seat A2, front aisle, in the all-economy, little propeller-aircraft. The ninety-minute flight was full service, so we did have some sort of breakfast. We were going to be half-board on the train, so this meal was instead of lunch.

I was first out of the aircraft at Victoria Falls and quickly but carefully filled out my visa. I was a bit nervous, as it was only recently that Zimbabwe had essentially reopened for tourism, but everything went well. All the luggage was taken by hand by the hard-working airport staff—there were no luggage carousels here! It was all fairly efficient though.

I was met by a lady holding a sign with my name. She suggested I grabbed a coffee, as she could see that the other family who were on the same flight as me were in a bit of a queue. Thirty minutes or so later, the other lovely family were introduced to me and we caught the minibus to the train. We all got to know each other during the journey. The family were originally from the UK but now lived in South Africa and had been on the train before. It was a really exciting journey across a rough road; I saw zebra and giraffes. It was kind of surreal, but gave such a great start to the trip, and we were not even on safari at this stage! Almost all the roads were rough there.

I was greeted on the train and had a chat with the train manager. There were only about thirty of us on board, so everyone got to know each other over the trip. I was taken to my cabin and given the good news that I'd been upgraded due to the train not being full. I now had an en-suite cabin, which was great news.

I was then taken to the actual Victoria Falls and pointed in the right direction for a lovely walk by the falls. I encountered some baboons, which were really cool—I like monkey-type animals. The falls were great and interesting. I then went to see the craft sellers, who were friendly but quite persistent, mainly due to the lack of tourists. I bought a wooden sculpture of the Big Six, which I really liked. Nothing was expensive; I don't think I even haggled.

Back on the train, we had a meeting explaining how everything worked and setting a few ground rules, like only having quick showers to ensure the hot water didn't run out. They also let us know that the cold tap water was good to drink and things like that. We were in the lounge carriage for this talk. There was a nice wee bar and all the drink was incredibly good value.

Dining was amazing throughout the trip in the attractive restaurant. There was no choice, but everything was tasty. It was a single service during our trip, but for some other trips they would have a first and second sitting. Early in the holiday, I got to know most of the passengers. There were a few South Africans, Brits, Australians, Dutch and Germans, and one Mexican lady.

I didn't sleep at all well the first night, possibly partially just due to excitement, but I got up ok the next day. That day, we were crossing the border into Zambia. We visited craft markets there, but it was mainly about seeing Victoria Falls from the Zambian side. It seemed more spectacular from this side. Some folk (not from our group) did something dangerous and bathed in a rockpool area with almost a sheer drop! This was near rainbow falls where, due to how the falls work, it always rains there and there's always a cute mini-rainbow! This was amazing.

The next day, we had a trip to Botswana. Rather than using the train's minibuses, we were met by a mini-fleet of open-top jeeps and Land Rovers. It was just a short drive to a small town by the Chobe River and we were taken to a luxury hotel. There, we had a buffet lunch, which was fantastic and only about ten or fifteen pounds. I never had an expensive meal at lunch, but typically ate very well! The setting here was great—stunning views of the river. I could even see wildlife from the decked seating area!

We then took a river cruise and saw crocodiles and hippos amongst loads of other wildlife and lots of different varieties of bird.

After this we were back in the open-top 4x4s, now doing a safari trek. This was amazing. It was rich with wildlife—we saw lions, rhinos, buffalo and elephants, and loads of everything. A sad but fascinating sight was watching hundreds of vultures (which are huge and creepy in person) picking away at what was left of a dead elephant! I was totally in awe of this safari day—it was just unbelievable!

Another new day, another new experience, and we went to Antelope Park. On arrival, our group was met by a guy with a missing arm! We listened really attentively to his safety briefing—and yes, he lost his arm in a lion-related incident! Sadly, the children, who were aged between eleven and fourteen, were all not tall enough to go on the lion walk. The rest of us chose a good stick each! Our safety brief was to approach the lion from behind—to do with dominance—handy to know this?!

We were then introduced to a handsome young lion. I think he was two or three and was a lovely animal. We went on a walk with him for fifty minutes or so. We stopped at the halfway point for ten minutes, and he sat with us. We were able to stroke him at this stage! This was some experience and I would say this was the highlight of the trip!

On arriving back at the main area, we watched a film about what they were trying to achieve through the breeding project. They also shared the exciting news that there was going to be an ITV1 documentary (in fact, there were a few series commissioned). Some of the people I met I later saw on TV.

We then went to the pen where the baby lions were and got to interact with them. Again, it was an amazing experience. I signed up for two more experiences, as we had now done the core ones. I was the only person there for the first one, which was a fascinating mini-tour of all the other lions. Many of the group opted for horse-riding. I then went on a walk with the elephant. This was not a ride on it, but a good walk with one of the rangers. A German lady joined me for this.

The next day, we visited Zimbabwe's second city, Bulawayo. This was again not too far a drive. On getting there, we visited a history museum, which was interesting. Then we went to a local hotel for lunch, another nice buffet. What was interesting was that none of the hotels accepted debit cards and there were no, or very few, local ATM cash machines. I was well prepared in any case and had enough US dollars with me.

In the afternoon, we went to the railway museum. Nothing was pristine there, and I liked this originality and authenticity.

The next day was a Zimbabwe game drive. This was to Hwange National Park. In advance of the trip, we were briefed that it would be much more spartan than the Botswana one.

I loved the classic 1970s fleet of Land Rovers waiting for us. We actually did quite well and saw a lot of the "Big Six", as they are known. We had to look harder to spot them, but the scenery was great. We stopped at a nice private resort for a BBQ lunch. Again, wild lions were the highlight here.

We also visited a local school. The kids sang and danced and did a talk. I gave away about five Dumbarton tops and the teachers and pupils were delighted. The school had a connection with railway workers. It was a lovely, happy experience.

The next day, we went to the Great Zimbabwe Monument. We were given a briefing before we went, telling us to be careful about what we said as the people there were big supporters of the president, Robert Mugabe. We went on a nice walk up a big hill and saw a number of monuments and statues. The history was very interesting. We learned more about David Livingstone's connections with Zimbabwe.

The next day brought a new country, Swaziland. On arrival, most of us survived passport control, but there were a few casualties, including the train's cleaner, as the floor had been waxed and was as slippery as an ice rink! Nobody was seriously injured, thankfully.

Our first stop was at a craft centre and I ended up buying a lion-type canvas. I enjoyed the countryside, but sadly, AIDS had caused really low life expectancy here. We went to a nice outdoor theatre and enjoyed a local cultural show. I found my time here really interesting!

Yet again, another day, another country, and we arrived in Maputo, Mozambique. We were told to be more careful about taking photos here. The train station was stunning—possibly the nicest train station I've ever been to! All the architecture in this city was stunning colonial. Our guide/driver was stopped by the police. We didn't think she'd done anything wrong; apparently it's common there just to be fined on the spot and not understand what you're meant to have done. She said it was best just to pay the fine. The family I met at the start of the trip very kindly offered to take me to lunch, knowing my love of seafood. This was very kind of them. They actually owned the train, and I discovered this round about this time. We went to an exclusive restaurant and all enjoyed a fresh seafood platter with amazing local beers!

Another day, another border crossing, and we were headed for South Africa. Mainly we spent this day on the train; the only day of the trip like that, and it was packed with incidents! First, a stationmaster alerted the train to say he saw stowaways by the train's bogies—a very dangerous thing to do, although the train rarely goes more than about thirty miles per hour. We had to pull in at this station and there was paperwork to do. We were there for about ninety minutes, but it was nice to just stretch our legs on the platform, which we were free to do.

After leaving this station for as little as thirty minutes, our engine came grinding to a halt. We had a few locomotive changes. Generally, the locomotive belonged to the railway of the country we were in. What appeared to have happened is someone had climbed onto the loco, James Bond style, and stole copper connections, as they were valuable. I am probably not describing this correctly, but it was along those lines!

The third incident happened literally as we were waiting for our starters to arrive in the restaurant carriage. It felt like the same incident as above, but some of the staff jumped out of their seats and told us we had derailed. It didn't feel at all bad, but the train staff were very anxious. The main thing was that everyone was ok and neither the loco nor the carriages overturned. We carried on with dinner and then went to the bar after the meal like usual. We were told that it was ok to get out of the train and have a look at what was going on. We were then told that, in the morning, the minibuses—which were in a special transporter carriage—would be used for at least the next day but possibly beyond that, and we would spend at least one night in a hotel by Kruger.

The next day, after an early breakfast, we had a lot of driving in front of us. The roads were scenic and, being in South Africa, they were proper sealed roads, so it was not a bumpy drive. After hours, it was a relief to get to Pilgrim's Rest, which was a really freaky pioneer place. It was a gold mine town and had a really interesting history, and is now a museum town full of interesting shops and experiences. The reason I say it was freaky is that there were kids in costumes deliberately scaring folk, for some kind of reason relating to the history of the place. They made funny, creepy noises. I did enjoy the time there and it was nice to have a break and get out of the minibuses.

We then saw a viewpoint of God's Window, which

is a canyon-type place, and there were stunning views here!

It was good to arrive at our hotel, and I was pleased it was one that I'd previously come across through work. We enjoyed a lovely meal at the restaurant.

After breakfast the next morning, there was the option to pay extra and do a safari trip in a jeep, or just stick to the minibus. Having done the jeeps in Botswana and Zimbabwe, I was totally happy just to stick to the minibus. Was a great day in the public game park in Kruger, which is huge—about two hours' drive in a straight line, observing the speed limits in place to ensure no animals are run over by vehicles. My highlight was seeing a leopard up a tree eating a dead cheetah. Morbid, I know, but it was very interesting and an unusual find— very hard to see. I had bought some binoculars for the trip, but I had to borrow higher-performance ones from a fellow traveller. I had no idea how they managed to spot this!

We went back to the hotel for a second night and had the most amazing BBQ dinner with everyone. The staff also performed songs and danced.

The next day, we drove through to pick up the train, which was back on the tracks. It was good to be back on the train. There were only two nights left.

Our last engine was actually a steam engine, which was a nice way to end the trip. We pulled into a siding, and it was actually a frosty start to the day—it was sort of winter in South Africa— but it was a sunny, fresh frost that was gone after breakfast.

I was excited to see some of the sites in Jo'burg. I visited the township where Nelson Mandela was from. I also visited one of the prisons he was in, and the Nelson Mandela Museum, which was very interesting. I also went to the church where Desmond Tutu had served, and another nearby museum that focused on the tragic Soweto Uprising, where seven hundred people lost their lives. It was quite a morbid day, but I believe learning more about these bad things is valuable educationally.

I enjoyed having lunch with my Australian friend. Just the two of us went to a shopping centre-type food court, and we both chose a seafood thing and shared a bottle of wine. Including the wine, the meal was the equivalent of about £10 each!

I haven't mentioned food too much in this write-up, mainly because I never wrote a journal, but the food was great—the train had a fantastic chef. We enjoyed exotic things like springbok (much like venison), buffalo, etc.

It's great that South Africa is now a democratic country. While it still has a lot of issues and there are dangerous places in the country, it has moved forward with equality and other important issues.

After a good last night's sleep, it was my last breakfast on the train and final day in South Africa. Today, we were given loads of choices. I chose fun and went to a smallish theme park. Didn't have much time there, and we stuck together as a small group of five or six. We went on a three- or four-G simulator, which was more for kids but was good fun. We did one or two other things, then it was off to a brewery for a tour and a quick lunch. Traffic was bad, and the brewery tour took longer than expected.

We packed, grabbed our suitcases, settled our bills and left our tips. Said bye to the lovely train crew, then headed to the airport.

On arrival at the airport, I was looking forward to a glass of champagne, but my airline's brand-new business-class lounge was on a soft opening and didn't yet have a liquor licence! Therefore, it was coffee and Coke only, but nice food!

Good flights back home and one of the airline sales team was also on my last flight from Dubai— it was nice to chat with her. However, an annoying couple were playing stuff out loud on a laptop, which was a pain!

This was my best ever holiday by a long way. For a few years, I stayed in touch with some of the people I met and had a sincere offer to stay at Leon and Derryn's (the train owners) house in South Africa for a few nights should I ever come back.

* * *

Not Quite Round the World!
Selling long-haul air tickets and holidays allowed me to see when good deals came up, and an amazing one did. I was able to do the following on one ticket for just £500, including airline taxes, etc. This was with about a £50 staff discount. Edinburgh – X London – X Bangkok – Phuket – Bangkok – Sydney – Auckland – X Sydney – X Singapore – Mumbai – X London – Edinburgh (X indicates a transit.)

This was with Qantas and British Airways, with internal Thailand flights on Bangkok Airways. I had big plans in Thailand, but my trip clashed with protests. The stops out and back helped break the journey up, as I wasn't really keen to go all the way to Australia nonstop! Essentially, two of the places in Thailand I was aiming to go to (Bangkok and Chiang Mai) were off limits due to protesters known as red and yellow shirts. All political stuff.

I was slightly nervous but I'd always wanted to go to Thailand. I had a good flight to Bangkok, and it's a good airport to transit. I would complete the customs checks in Phuket, so I was able to go straight to the Bangkok Airways lounge on arrival at Bangkok. This was a free lounge for all Bangkok Airways passengers; they are known as a boutique airline and really look after their passengers with high levels of service, even for economy passengers. The lounge was much like the service air lounge in Edinburgh. There were sandwiches and other snacks, tea and coffee, and some stuff to read. Had a nice free sandwich on the flight, too.

Immigration for international arrivals was really quiet in Phuket and took no time to clear, partly due to people not going to Thailand due to the protests. There were spectacular views of the islands and beaches during the flight. I was greeted by my driver with a sign with my name on it, and I was the only pick-up so it was a nice drive to my hotel, the Centara Karon resort, about forty minutes away.

This was a fantastic hotel. I had a nice welcome drink on arrival, and a friendly receptionist told me the good news that I was getting a free room upgrade and a free thirty-minute massage, together with other perks. The hotel was good value for food and drink, but I do like to eat where the locals eat, and the town centre was a five-minute walk from the hotel. There were massage parlours, restaurants and tailors. I chose an amazing place to dine. It was a seafood restaurant that had a live fish tank, and you could choose your fish and the style you wanted it cooked in. To start, I went for prawns in a garlic and ginger sauce, then for main, I had a crab dish. Beers were about £1 each. With the beers, this meal was only about £15—amazing for top-quality seafood!

Was glad of the dinner, but really tired after my international flight, so went off to bed!

Next morning, I heard someone knocking on my door. Thinking it was room service, I said I was still in bed, but the knocking persisted. Turned out to be a Russian (I think?) lady. She had somehow thrown an item of clothing—a bikini, I think?!?!—which had landed on my balcony. I was nervous, as I didn't have a clue what she was saying. She didn't speak any English, and my Russian language skills weren't too good either! Eventually, after loads of miming, I returned her item! This was at about 9 a.m., so I showered and headed for breakfast, which was a quite good mix of Western and Asian food.

The main thing on this day was a pre-booked elephant excursion. This was amazing; the animals looked well cared for, and the handlers were gentle, friendly but quite shy (they are known as mahouts). The trek was great and over interesting streams and jungle for a decent length of time. We stopped at a village to look at crafts and things before taking the elephant back to the base. We then enjoyed a nice Thai lunch, and I went for my hotel massage. Then I took a walk around the town, before heading back to the hotel for happy hour!

The hotel bar was really cool, with four-poster-bed-type seats! I asked for a piña colada, which was actually served inside a coconut! When I finished, the free one arrived, to my surprise, as it was happy hour—buy-one-get-one-free! Was about four pounds for the two, and they were probably the nicest-presented cocktails I've had to date!

Next day was a trip round the island that was really interesting. First stop was a viewpoint, then a temple, then a factory outlet-type souvenir place, then lunch, then a diamond factory. With lunch, this trip was only about £12. I think the diamond place and souvenir place really subsidise the trip.

I went back to the hotel, then headed for a local massage, which was amazing—quite tough going, too, as Thai massages are very firm. It was only about ten pounds for one hour! Then dinner was at the Green Tomato restaurant. This place had high ratings on TripAdvisor and was good and cheap, but not as nice as the place the previous night.

Next day was a leisurely trip to the airport—I had chosen sensible flight times. Hotel gave me complimentary refreshments while I waited for the transfer. This used to be one of my best-selling hotels, and I was so impressed!

Short flight back to Bangkok, and the friendly driver told me that the transfer to Pattaya Hotel would be about ninety minutes. It ended up being closer to an hour, which was great.

Hotel reception at the Pullman hotel was stunning. There was a friendly welcome with a refreshing welcome drink. Again, I sold myself this five-star hotel. The room was very dated but ok.

There was a tuk-tuk free shuttle into the centre area. I found a nice seafood restaurant with an amazing view on Walking Street Pattaya. I enjoyed a lovely seafood platter, then attempted to get back to the hotel, only to see the hotel tuk-tuk (last one of the night) pulling away five minutes early. After my thirty-minute walk back to the hotel in hot and humid night weather, I complained to reception.

After breakfast, which was very similar to the other hotel's, I went to the hotel's beach for a bit.

It was really nice. Hotel had a French feel about it. After a few hours, I headed back for a nap, but there was refurbishment work and all I could hear was the hammer banging away! I went to reception, who moved me to a floor away from the noise.

In the evening I tried taking the tuk-tuk again and decided on a restaurant not far from where it dropped me. I had an amazing Thai green curry. Again, very cheap. Back at the hotel, I noticed ants everywhere in my room, and this time I was upgraded as well as moved, but the staff acted as if there was nothing much wrong with this?!

I skipped breakfast the next day as I was off to a cookery school. The host told me that, due to the conflicts, I was the first student they'd had in a few months. It was a great experience and she helped me learn how to make some lovely dishes. I ate all the food I made—I really like Thai food. I enjoyed the beach in the afternoon and headed to a bar in the evening.

Next day, I went to the tiger breeding project. The conditions weren't great, but I could see they were helping preserve endangered and stunning animals. For extra money, there were photo opportunities with baby and adult tigers, the adult clearly sedated. There were also elephants and crocodiles and various shows. I enjoyed it here, but at the same time, something about it felt not quite right.

In the evening, I enjoyed another massage and then had dinner at the hotel. There was a seafood and wine night, with unlimited seafood, all the usual stuff—lobster, oysters, prawns in shells, mussels, etc. It was great and, for about twenty pounds, it was amazing. Ordinarily, the wine alone sold for thirty pounds or more. Imported wine is really expensive at most hotels and restaurants in Thailand.

Another new day, and this one was a city tour. I saw Jomtien Beach, a temple and new places. The tour was heavily sponsored by the diamond factory, and to at least buy something, I got something really cheap—a candle set for five pounds.

After an early dinner at a nearby Korean restaurant, I headed to the airport, as I was flying to Sydney.

I enjoyed my time in Thailand—lovely hotel but not without issues. It was quite full-on. Walking Street was eye-opening, as were many of the courtyard-type bars.

Next up was my fourth trip to Sydney. I won't go into huge detail, as I've already covered Sydney quite extensively. I stayed at the Arts Hotel (previously known as Sullivan's) and its sister hotel in Perth, which was nice. They are friends with my previous employer and, as such, always encouraged us to stay with them when in Sydney or Perth. It was in a leafy suburb, but I still found it ok to walk into the city centre from there. Prior to my trip, I spoke to a rep from Tourism Australia, who was from Sydney, for some ideas of what to do, given that I'd already seen the main highlights.

He suggested Doyle's on the beach, getting the ferry from Circular Quay and having a nice fish and chips. This was great, although the sit-in was shut, but the take-away was an amazing fish supper. I was happily sat on a park bench, watching the sea, which worked out well.

I also did a trip to Hunter Valley for amazing wine-tasting. This was a great experience with lunch and also a beer-tasting paddle, as well as three vineyards. Our group had a brilliant guide!

The weather was actually really cool—almost cold, like a UK autumn day—as it was winter in Sydney. That's all I'll say about Sydney, but it is without a doubt one of my favourite places in the world!

Auckland was much the same as Sydney in terms of a repeat visit. It was just a one-night/two-day stay. I came back here essentially just to go back to Waiheke Island, probably my favourite place I've ever been to!

At Auckland Airport, something funny happened when I went to the Qantas desk to check in for Mumbai. The lovely check-in lady said, "How can you be leaving? You never actually arrived!" There was a processing error. She was very apologetic, and I found it funny! She handed me three boarding cards as I was transiting both Sydney and Singapore. I was given business class between Singapore and Mumbai and told I could also use the business-class airport lounges in both Sydney and Singapore.

The first flight, Auckland to Sydney, was fine, but my flight to Singapore was delayed by about an hour. The one before mine was delayed even longer—if I'd been on the earlier one, I would have actually missed my connection! I understood that, because both flights were full, people couldn't switch to mine. I made my connection just before the gates closed, no time to use the Singapore Qantas airport lounge. The lady greeted me off the flight and whisked me over to get on my connection, which pretty much left right away. I was worried my checked luggage wouldn't make it, but it did!

Business class was ok—not as good as Emirates, but I was well looked after and there was plenty of champagne. Food was ok, definitely better than economy. Guy next to me was friendly as well.

On arriving at Mumbai, the great news was that my luggage made it. I found the taxi desk and promptly got into my yellow and black (Dumbarton colours!) Tata taxi, which looked like a 1960s Austin, but I was told these cars were actually mostly about ten to fifteen years old. Tata makes cars like Maestros! Why would you?

The taxi driver couldn't find my hotel. The journey was interesting and eye-opening, as we passed some slum areas and saw some people living in their cars, etc. It wasn't easy at all. After about an hour and a half, we found my hotel, which was right by Crawford Market, one of the main tourist attractions in the city, especially famous for buying live animals. Taxi was only about six pounds—such a long journey would have been fifty pounds plus in most countries!

Hotel must have had the world's oldest lift! It was one of the ones where you have to close the weird metal bar thing. It worked but freaked me out. The room at the two-star hotel was mega small, but it had effective air-con, hot water, and en-suite. My sister told me that the combination I've described is rare. She also warned me that her experience in India was that the taxis would try to take you to their friend/relative's hotel instead if you booked somewhere cheap. I think mine was about thirty-five pounds B&B per night. I slept ok— it was fairly soundproof. I was a bit freaked out, though, as in the communal areas by the roof, I could see several eyes looking through the ceiling cracks. Staff appeared to live in a bit where there wasn't even a proper ceiling—couldn't be at all comfortable, maybe slightly better than the slums.

The next morning, I got up and went to the café

next door, which was part of my hotel and had a basic but ok breakfast: tea, toast and omelette. Then, after breakfast, the heavens opened; there was so much rain. Managed to get a brolly from man with a wee street stall. The locals were so reactive and resourceful!

It only rained for a short while. I then got a taxi to the Gateway of India, possibly the most well-known attraction in Mumbai. I hadn't booked anything and loads of folk tried to sell me guided tours. They all seemed good value, but I had specific things I wanted to do, and today I wanted to go to Elephanta Island.

It was easy enough to find a passenger ferry. The ferry was interesting. I noticed I was the only Western passenger; this was a Saturday. The journey took about an hour each way and was comfortable enough on the basic ferry. Also, the caves were all closed, which is one of the highlights of the island. There was a structure on the island— not sure if it was a jail or something.

On arrival, the pier was long and there was an abandoned mini-railway train and track, which probably hadn't run for years. I enjoyed just having a wander around. There were nice walks in hills and woods-type settings. After wandering about for a few hours, I found a restaurant and choose "lunch" from the menu. There were lots of different options, but one simply said "lunch". Like around half the restaurants in Mumbai, this one was a vegetarian one. Lunch was great—a massive silver platter with about eight sections, which came with poppadum, chapatti, rice, dhal and lots of different curries and sides. It was just a few pounds, like most places there. The restaurant was very quiet—I think I was the only customer.

Headed back to the ferry after this. On the way, I came across a few goats butting each other, which I found very funny.

I got back to the hotel, found an off-licence-type place and bought two huge bottles of Kingfisher beer. Then I did something really bad! I went into autopilot, momentarily forgot what country I was in, and drank from the bottle! I immediately noticed the fishy smell, and oh no! There was almost certainly rat's urine on the outside of the bottle.

I still drank the next bottle, but by pouring the beer into the glass in my room. I felt ok, although on returning back to the UK, I had horrific rat poisoning for about ten nights!

After a couple of hours, I decided to have dinner at the restaurant in my hotel. Again, it was a separate building but part of the hotel. It was an impressive, really funky, attractive place with young people smoking the hubba bubba and really modern décor. I had a brilliant meal here—goat curry. It wasn't dear, although it was double the price of most places—two courses with three beers was about ten pounds all in. I had some sort of sweetcorn curry as my starter, which was amazing.

After another good sleep and breakfast, I got a taxi to the zoo. I found it funny that there were three ticket prices: local people, Western people and cameras. Cameras were dearest! Wasn't expensive, but there weren't many animals. Quite nice grounds, though, and wasn't too busy! Had a good look round the market next to my hotel after this—all the live animals for sale were amazing. Found a local restaurant for dinner, which was fine. I had mutton curry and again it was tasty and very cheap.

Next day was spent getting the taxi to the airport

and flying back home after the end of another great adventure.

* * *

Dubai

My next industry trip was when I won two return flights to Dubai due to my Emirates sales performance, and I managed to get an amazing deal at Raffles Dubai, which is the same hotel chain as the famous Singapore Raffles. I took my mum with me. Having been to Dubai before, I won't talk too much about this trip, but the hotel was amazing—definitely one of my favourite hotels I've ever stayed at. This was my mum's first time in Dubai.

Main highlights were visiting the huge shopping centre with the huge indoor ski slope, doing the city tour with a lovely dinner cruise following it, and having a really authentic Arabian meal the following evening. Due to flight times, it was a two-and-a-half-night trip. One thing I liked at the hotel was that, before going to bed on the last night, I booked an alarm call and the very helpful receptionist told me he would send complimentary coffee and shortbread the following morning.

I've been to Dubai twice to stay and transited it two or three times, too. It's an interesting place; the level of wealth is amazing.

Thailand

I won a competition at work from the Starwood Group for luxury hotel accommodation in Thailand. Was an amazing prize and, coincidently, I was actually holding almost the same destinations as this was going to be my next trip—what were the chances! I had also moved away from sales at work to more online support, so there had been fewer opportunities for prizes like this.

My trip, again with Emirates, started really well, as I had enough frequent flyer loyalty points to upgrade Glasgow-Dubai to business class. This even got me the free limousine, which is always a great way to start a trip!

I started with three nights at the Royal Orchid Sheraton. After a tough arrival due to what felt like a never-ending immigration queue, it was good to get my transfer and a fairly smooth journey to my central Bangkok hotel. I was greeted by one of the senior hotel managers with a petal garland; it was a nice touch for him to personally welcome me. I had a lovely room and was on a B&B basis throughout my Thai hotels. This was a fantastic hotel and I was on something like the sixteenth floor. Amazing coffee and breakfasts, as in all the Starwood hotels.

The next morning after breakfast, my tour guide arrived to take me to the Grand Palace. This was an amazing and interesting place. After being dropped off, I headed to the night market and bought a few Thai ties! Also, a candle scent thing. I went to a street food-type place for dinner, which was really nice and authentic.

The next day, I went around some temples, again with a tour guide. There was the Temple of the Reclining Buddha, the Golden Buddha and another one. These were interesting, but too similar a tour to that of the Grand Palace.

I then took the short Bangkok Air flight to Phuket. This time, I was staying at the brand-new Westin Siray Bay, which had incredible sea views—it was built on a clifftop. It was a stunning hotel. I had an amazing seafood dinner one night and ate in a local restaurant on the second night. It was a totally different part of the island to my last trip and it was good to see other areas. There was an amazing swim-up bar at the hotel. I liked that. If staff saw you walking, they would pick you up on their electric golf-type buggies and take you where you wanted to go.

Next stop was Le Meridien Khao Lak—I think this hotel is now part of another group. I loved this place, it was like a mix of rainforest and beach. It was so relaxing, although on my first night, I was a bit freaked out by lights going on and off as if there was a ghost! Probably some sort of electrical issue. I had a mini-suite here, a stunning room in just a total paradise place. Was about an hour and a half's drive from my Phuket hotel, with a bridge connecting to Phuket.

Next up was my favourite place I've ever been to in Thailand, Chiang Mai! Again, I was staying at Le Meridien—such a classy hotel chain. I think all the Le Meridiens are five-star hotels, and you can really see the French chic ambiance of the properties.

Despite being a high-rise hotel, it felt lovely. It was right in the centre of Chiang Mai next to the most amazing night market, both for shops and food. I had one of my best meals in Thailand at the food market. You bought tokens from a stall, then used these at the cashless food stalls—it was so cool and a great system. I had the most amazing seafood starters and mains, with some nice local beers and ice cream for dessert. Three courses and three beers came to about ten pounds, and that was with expensive choices!

The next day was amazing—went to another

elephant trek at a sort of elephant refuge. On the way, I stopped at an orchid garden centre place and, after the amazing elephant experience, went on a river trip, which was uncomfortable as there was no proper seat! Was really glad to finish that!

I was pleased to get back to the hotel for a nice swim in the outdoor rooftop pool! Dinner that night was part of a sightseeing trip. It was the cultural show and banquet – a great excursion that came in at about ten pounds including transfers! You were given a huge silver meze tray with about twelve different types of food, enough for about four or five people! The show was amazing and lasted a good few hours.

Loved my time in Chiang Mai. Next stop was back to the same hotel in Pattaya as I'd stayed in last time I was in Thailand—The Pullman. This time, I was in a luxury club room, which was only about an extra ten pounds a night. That gave me access to the exclusive and luxurious club lounge. This was an amazing room, never overly busy, and was more of a premium breakfast experience with better quality food. Also, I was able to enjoy drinks that had been out-of-range elsewhere in Thailand due to export taxes. Wine and gin are awfully dear in Thailand for this reason—typically, a house bottle of wine can easily be thirty pounds. Almost any type of drink was free for over an hour every night to club room guests! Was a fantastic stay here, and I understood Pattaya better this time.

This was an amazing trip. Reminiscing does make me miss being a travel agent, although I do still have a travel-related sideline.

* * *

Canada – Victoria Island, Vancouver and Toronto

I had gone to a Tourism Canada presentation for travel agents in Glasgow and had also completed a thirty-plus-hour online course to become an accredited Canada travel expert. The event was amazing. For a start, it was held at the stunning WEST brewery in Glasgow Green, which was a former factory and is a lovely terracotta-coloured building. The beer there is great too! After going round all the regional stalls, there was a group presentation and then there was a draw for travel agent familiarisation trips, known as "fam trips". Winners all had to be accredited Canada experts. I was one of the very lucky agents. This was only a month after I had moved from an employed to a self-employed position.

I was even given a choice of which parts to go to. Despite doing my course, I felt from an industry point of view that it was important to personally get to know the two biggest cities as first priority, hence choosing Vancouver and Toronto. Well, everyone went to Toronto, as we all met up together as a group there.

This was an autumn trip in September and "the fall", as it's known in Canada, was really spectacular with the change of leaves on the trees. Our flight was a bit late leaving Heathrow, and we just missed our connection, but the good news was that the flights to Victoria (Vancouver Island) were pretty regular, roughly hourly, and despite there being about seven of us in the group, Air Canada managed to get us all into the next flight. We had tried to inform our transfer company of our delay but hadn't managed to get hold of them. After getting our luggage, I noticed a minibus with the transfer company name just leaving—turned out they had picked up the wrong people! No matter, I took control and sorted a public airport transfer bus. A funny thing happened on the bus. A man wearing First Nation clothing asked my new friend, Alan, to smell his book—I had a sniff too! Smelt of burning wood! That was just an unusual scenario.

We were a good two or so hours late checking into the hotel but still managed our first activity, which was a trip to the landmark Fairmont Hotel. This was one of the most stunning hotels, inside and out, I'd ever seen. It was a real privilege to visit.

After this came a good night's sleep.

After a lovely Canadian breakfast, we headed for a city tour and then whale-watching. I was incredibly lucky to see about fifty orcas (killer whales). This was an incredible experience! It was actually a Scottish lady who hosted us for this. In the afternoon, we headed to Butchart Gardens, which was also stunning—one of the nicest gardens I've seen. Had a lovely hosted dinner at an amazing seafood restaurant! We went for a drink after this at a lovely wee pub. I loved my short stay at Vancouver Island and recommend this place to anyone!

After breakfast the next day, we headed to the bus station, as we were taking the ferry to Vancouver. This leisurely three-hour journey took in some stunning scenery—reminded me a lot of the islands off the west coast of Scotland! Exiting the ferry, we had a lovely hour-long run into the city centre. I loved all the pumpkin fields we encountered.

On arriving into the city centre, we met our guide and headed to the crafty Granville Island, which is like a permanent farmers' market and lovely food and craft stalls hosted in some stunning buildings. It was lovely just to browse these. We then did a short harbour cruise and dinner was at a contemporary restaurant.

We had breakfast at the prettiest boutique hotel—the Wedgewood. I totally loved it, such a lovely place. Then we headed to the aquarium. I loved the beluga whales, although sadly, one of them died the day after we were there. We then went over the Capilano Suspension Bridge, which was an amazing experience, even with a slight fear of heights. Think a big, scaled-up bridge from *I'm a Celebrity, Get Me Out of Here*! Went on a lovely treetop walk too, then took the cable car to Grouse Mountain.

Our last day here was more leisurely. After a nice breakfast, we did a cycle trip, which was flat, car-free and a very nice way to explore round a lake. Then we headed to fly to Toronto and got access to the Air Canada lounge, which was good.

It was late by the time we got to Toronto, so we pretty much went to bed when we got to the hotel. The next morning at breakfast it was nice to catch up with all the other groups—we were all to meet up for the last two days. We then headed to the bus going to Niagara Falls. Got soaked on the Falls boat trip and I think that contributed to me catching a cold the day after the trip.

Next up was a helicopter trip over the Falls; this was an amazing experience. I was really impressed with the organisation of the operation! Seeing the Falls from above was amazing! First time in a helicopter too! We then headed to a vineyard tour and lunch. I loved the vineyard and the ice wines were especially special and unique. Then off for a wander round Niagara by the lake—so pretty. Had an amazing coffee here!

The bus back was good fun, as I caught up with

my friend John, who had been on the Quebec and Montreal itinerary. I will definitely go there when I next visit Canada! We had dinner at the revolving tower restaurant. Loved the views, but the food and service were not in the least bit special.

The next day, each of the groups did a presentation and everyone had to contribute. This was great fun and was a very good idea. We then did a duck vehicle tour on both land and water, then went to a museum and shopping centre.

* * *

I will cover all my cruise experiences in the next chapter. I have had some special cruise ship agent lunch visits and also attended a special cruise travel agent conference in Southampton.

CHAPTER 10

All My Cruises

First trip on Cunard's QE2 back in the late 1990s. Cruise to nowhere!

The good thing about cruising is waking up to a new destination every day or two without having to pack and unpack and also the good quality food, all included.

My friend Jonathan had talked passionately about cruising. He likes the historic ships, and generally cruised either on the *QE2* or the *Norway* (previously known as the *France*) but generally avoids the modern ones. He talked me into it, and I'm glad he did, although my first experience was nearly my last!

This was meant to be a cruise to Jersey for three nights. I was so excited making my way down to Southampton. I probably was overdressed, thinking how regal and grand it would be, and I don't even think I had a pair of jeans.

Embarkation was fairly smooth and straightforward and it was really exciting to get on board. There was brass and wood everywhere—was totally stunning. I loved just wandering around the decks, both inside and out, like a resort at sea. In the 1960s this iconic Clyde-built ocean liner was once one of the biggest liners, but nowadays it would only be classed as a medium-sized ship. I found its size perfect. I also liked the fact there was a lovely chilled bottle of sparkling wine in my cabin—this is something you no longer see much of unless you're really high up the tiers for the cruise line's loyalty programme.

I kept comparing it to the Orient Express, but you can't really compare a luxury train with a luxury ship! The food was definitely better on the train, but it was still very good on the ship. I wasn't impressed with my table back then, but today I would probably have found it interesting. I was sharing a table with four gentleman hosts. I think I didn't like the fact they were not regular paying passengers.

I enjoyed the shops, including Harrods at sea, the swimming pool, the deck games like shuffleboard, the bars and the entertainment, including a lovely casino.

Unfortunately, arriving at Jersey, there was a muffled announcement that I never heard and other staff weren't really able to clarify. The ship was anchored, as the port didn't have a big enough jetty or the water was too shallow. I went to the meeting point, dressed for autumnal weather like a fool, as I hadn't understood we were not getting ashore!

This ended up being a cruise to nowhere and I wasn't at all impressed with the communication. I ended up getting a small credit towards my next Cunard trip, either £50 or £100. This was probably the only reason I went back on another one.

Second trip on QE2, a nice cruise to Norway for around a fortnight.
Norway was having record temperatures and the destinations were stunning. The fact it was for a decent period of time was great. I met some really nice people and got on really well with a Morton-supporting fellow, Hugh, whose son was a kid on Rangers' books. Enjoyed table tennis and shuffleboard with Hugh. I loved the places on this trip. Cruising here was great as you could get to see lovely locations without spending a fortune on eating/drinking out.

Stavanger – This is the oil capital of Norway and had lovely tourism places, such as a folk museum and the fantastic oil museum, which was very interesting and something totally different. Also had a £5 half-pint here, and this was almost twenty years ago—service wasn't even great!

Oslo – Loved it here, was on a bus tour. Loved the sculpture park, the palace, the Viking museum. Had a great guide, which made the experience. Also went on a harbour cruise. Remortgaged my flat to buy a lovely ice cream— glad it was worth it!

Geiranger – Amazing fjord experience through the twisting and turning fjords, just stunning scenery.

Bergen – Enjoyed the lovely wooden buildings

hosting bars, shops and the occasional house. Took a cable car up a hill and enjoyed the fish market.

This trip hooked me and cruising in the future was a certainty!

Fred Olsen's Braemar, good to try another cruise line. This was a trip to Amsterdam, I think, over about three nights.

I had lovely younger people at my dinner table whom I socialised with in the evening, great company. I really liked a delightful lady who worked at my favourite London Underground station—Earl's Court! Really liked the food and was close to the standard of Cunard.

Fred Olsen has a Norwegian heritage but is known as a British cruise experience. Was a lovely, light ship. This was the first outside cabin I'd had. My previous two trips were inside cabins, which were not all negative. I found one of the positives was a good quiet sleep. I actually sleep better in an inside rather than outside cabin.

MSC Cruises Melody. A very interesting cruise on the Mediterranean.

A great story about this trip is that it cost me ten pounds! I just had to get to London Gatwick. This was thanks to an offer where if you collected fifty different Daily Express tokens, you got a cruise for ten pounds. It was amazing to get the cruise for so little.

On embarkation, I was shown to my cabin and, unbelievably, I had somehow been upgraded to a mini-suite. I had a separate lounge and bedroom and daily replenished fruit bowl! Again, another great, fun table, and seven-course dinners! Food was quite good.

Destinations were:

Naples – Enjoyed a "hop-on hop-off" bus tour and eating a pizza from the place that invented pizza!

Tunisia – Too full-on for me. Vendors really were pests and browsing the stalls did feel like an obligation! I did like the pretty blue and white buildings in Sidi Bou Said.

Valetta, Malta – This was a stunning walled city with amazing cathedrals and history going back to the Knights Templar. I have returned to Valetta numerous times in the last few years!

Ibiza Town – Didn't go far, just a walk over by the promenade, but it looked really nice.

Milan – A chic city square. You could tell this was a highly fashionable Italian city.

What a great cruise for just ten pounds! Don't think I will ever get an offer like this again, but it was genuine, as everybody who collected got a trip, as far as I was aware.

Celebrity Cruise's Century. This was a transatlantic trip, Barcelona to Miami, in autumn 2006.

This was a stunning cruise ship, the biggest one I had been on at that point. Was a very dramatic trip for very sad reasons. I had just left my long-standing job and this trip was to help me recharge my batteries before starting my new estate agency career. My gran had had a bad fall and had been really ill in hospital. She had just started making better progress, so after a discussion with my dad, Aunt Betty and my mum, I decided not to cancel my trip. I went to see my gran the afternoon before my trip and was pleased she was able to have a chat and seemed to be doing better. Sadly, the second night on board the ship, I got the phone call I was dreading, as my dad broke the news that she had died. I had always got on really well with my gran, who had really good understanding and empathy throughout my life.

Going back a day, the trip got off to another bad start. I had flagged my concern over a really tight connection in Heathrow. Before my trip, neither Celebrity or BA were interested, and I never had any choice with this connection. It was also a frosty morning and my BA shuttle to Heathrow had not been defrosted and, as such, was about an hour late, giving me about ten minutes to make my Barcelona flight! I made it, having had a very helpful stewardess letting me off first and giving me my new gate. They were actually waiting for me at the next gate, arriving at Barcelona, and I waited and waited at the carousel, but my luggage never arrived. I reported this to someone, who seemed unhelpful, but there was not much they could do. The Celebrity staff were also unhelpful, advising me I was holding up the last bus, and they wouldn't let me go and buy any clothes!

On getting on board, I was incredibly stressed out and very uncomfortable only really having what I was wearing. First thing I did after checking my lovely cabin was talk to the concierge team. The young man looked after me well, giving me new underwear and a few T-shirts. He told me not to worry about complying with dress code after I told him that I really didn't want to be forced to dine in the buffet as I much prefer cruise à la carte. I didn't feel comfortable and had to explain to everyone at my table. I was on a mixed table—I liked one of the couples and tolerated the others. There was an American celebrity on my table; he was a huge fellow and a senior CNN reporter who was unhappy that I didn't know who he was! He would have three deserts most nights and, on the lobster night, he had four full lobster meals!

I ended up being without luggage for three nights. Really had a bad impact on my experience and, with the sad news about my gran, this felt like a total nightmare of a cruise.

Thankfully, when I got my luggage at Nice, I started to feel I could enjoy it. I had dined buffet on nights two and three as I really didn't enjoy going to dinner in jeans and a T-shirt when the expectation was suit and tie.

The food was excellent and pretty decent in the buffet too. The ship was very elegant. People were taking the table tennis a bit too seriously—I think that was partly because of the nationality of the guests. The table tennis host demanded I repeatedly serve about ten times as he and my opponent thought I was serving illegally!!! I beat my opponent, then the host said my next opponent was much better than me! Meant to be on holiday. I did lose the next game, and that was me done with table tennis! I think I played the odd game of shuffleboard. I really enjoyed the casino here and got on well with a particular croupier who was very sympathetic about my lack of luggage. I also enjoyed the art auctions.

I enjoyed our next stop, Madeira, and now that things had calmed down, I was able to enjoy it more. I took the cable car up to the botanical gardens, which were lovely, and got the famous Monte basket ride back to the bottom, then a spot of Madeira tasting.

This was the last stop before arriving in Miami. I enjoyed my sea days. There was an excellent speaker on board, the late John Maxtone-Graham, whose passion for all things ship was great. I went to all his talks, and they were amazing. I learnt about other great ships and started to become more interested in other older ships. This inspired me to get on *Black Prince* before she was retired.

I particularly enjoyed the extra-cost fine dining restaurant, Murano. I had almost the same meal the three times I dined here. Foie gras, Russian salad, lobster and the cheese trolley, which was an incredible choice of about forty fine cheeses that were outstanding!

The bad things continued to happen. Firstly, a Scottish man from Burntisland jumped off halfway across the Atlantic. We did go back to try to find him, but like most of these situations, it would have been almost impossible to find him alive. Then two seriously ill passengers were transferred by zodiac boat between our ship and a huge US navy ship that met us in the middle of the Atlantic. Was quite a sight to see all the sailors, immaculate and saluting our ship—just a pity about the sad circumstances.

The last night, we were told that we would be late into Miami by about four or five hours, and also that the ship had run out of bread, butter, milk, sugar and a few other things. This was poor, and there was no excuse, as we never had extra meals. Probably didn't help that people like the man on my table had loads of extra portions!

The FBI boarded the ship in Miami, and we were delayed by another few hours. We were not really looked after well. Also, the final issue was when I swiped out, there was an alert! Turned out my credit card had been cloned and fraud attempted! Again, not well dealt with, but I've since been on a good cruise with the same line and, despite everything, I did enjoy this trip.

The good news is that I spoke to a British Airways manager about my poor experience flying out and wangled a premium economy (World Traveller Plus) flight to Edinburgh, and he also sorted me business class lounges in both Miami and Heathrow on the basis that I agreed to this being my airline complaint resolution!

Island Cruise's Island Escape – Palma, Majorca to Rio de Janeiro, Brazil.
This was the longest cruise I've ever done, just under three weeks and on quite a small ship. This ship had recently been on about half a dozen episodes of a TV series about the cruise ship experience. It had also recently been in the news because of sewage issues.

I took a charter half-empty First Choice flight from Edinburgh to Palma and then a smooth bus transfer to the ship. The friendly entertainment staff met us on arrival, and this was a good start.

I didn't like that only buffet meals were included, but the cruise was very good value, especially considering the destinations and that flights were included. I was also staying in a five-star hotel for the last two nights in Rio.

I liked that it was quite a small ship and really got to know a lot of folk, both staff and passengers. I met some lovely people on this trip. There were really two different groups of friends, one from the games—shuffleboard, table tennis, etc.—and one from the casino. I did quite well at the casino here. This was a fun cruise; it wasn't about high quality but was about making an effort and going with the flow, and it was the most fun and involved cruise I've ever done. I had an amazing time. Among the more unusual destinations was Cape Verdi, which was quite under construction but still somewhat interesting.

The Brazilian destinations were varied. I didn't much like Salvador, and we were told to be careful there and try not to look too much like tourists. I think this made me more worried than I should have been, as I did enjoy a trip to a fish market where you bought the food direct from the fishermen then had it prepared and cooked at café-type stalls. I also liked the coconut-water sellers who would open the coconut for you—this was delicious.

I really liked Fortaleza, which had a lot of history, and went on a good sightseeing day to old forts out there. Had a lovely steak lunch there, every bit as good as Angus steak!

I loved Bùzios as well—stunning beaches and a pretty town centre.

The hotel in Rio didn't feel as good as the five-star hotels I was used to but it was ok. I was quite lucky to get a five-star as some other guests were in three- and four-star hotels, and I never paid any supplement to guarantee this. My hotel was on the Copacabana beach, which was a bonus—I did enjoy going into the beachside bars and restaurants. My favourite sightseeing here was Christ the Redeemer. I really enjoyed the mountain railway train up there through a mini rainforest. I also did the cable car to Sugar Loaf Mountain.

I felt so relaxed on this cruise that I made an attempt at stand-up comedy in front of an audience of about a thousand people. I coped ok and managed to get through my act to a reasonable reception!

Fred Olsen's Black Prince. Mini-cruise, Greenock – Dublin — Liverpool

I loved this ship, especially the history, as it dates back to about 1964. However, my first cabin was too close to the nightclub and was crazy noisy! Managed to get a change of cabin, though.

Met some nice folk, particularly on my dinner table. We socialised together after dinner and went to quizzes and other things like that. This was down as a two-star cruise, but it was one of my favourite ships I've been on and also the smallest. Enjoyed Dublin, went around on the "hop-on hop-off" bus with a stop and tour of the Guinness storehouse.

Third trip on QE2

This was for just under a fortnight in 2009. I would say this was my favourite cruise ever! This was intended to be my last *QE2* cruise and was one of the ship's final cruises, but because I enjoyed it so much and got a reasonable deal, I then went back on about the third-last cruise this ship ever did!

For this one, I can't remember all the destinations, but it included places like Nice and Gibraltar.

The main highlight of this trip was being at the captain's table. On any formal nights, we were hosted by the captain or one of the officers. We particularly enjoyed the security officer Michael's company. He was happy to host us in the bars or clubs after dinner. It was just great to be on a table with such great company. I got on really well with a lot of my table and stayed in touch with Deborah from near Southampton until about five years ago. I'm still in touch with Stewart after all these years, exchanging text messages every now and again. The dining was superb and the entertainment on Cunard is the best, from the cruise director and entertainment team to the singers and dancers.

Final cruise on QE2. This was to Nice, Bordeaux and Guernsey over four nights.
Having only been able to get a twin cabin, I enquired what the supplement would be to add my mum to my booking. It was very low, as solo travellers in twin cabins pay almost double, sometimes even more than double. This gave my mum the chance to sail on *QE2* before it retired. Following this trip, Mum has never looked back, and for the last few years, has done parts of the world cruise and has done Cunard's *QM2* transatlantic New York crossing and Alaska! This was another great cruise. Due to jumping at a cancellation, I luckily managed to secure this at a very fair price.

MSC Cruises Opera Baltic cruise. Southampton – Amsterdam – Tallinn (Estonia) – St Petersburg (Russia) for two nights — Copenhagen (Denmark) – Hamburg (Germany) – Southampton.
Another MSC trip in an attractive, modern, large ship. My cabin was bright and attractive. There were nice folk on my table but only three of us— Anne, Lorena and me. The destinations were really good. Tallinn was easily my favourite, a stunning medieval city that really reminded me of York, with ye olde worlde cobbled streets and fantastic museums! Went to places like the Church of the Saviour on Spilled Blood in St Petersburg, which was stunning. This is the (ice-cream-shaped) domed building. Did find the locals somewhat cold and secretive.

The most disappointing thing about this trip was the food. There was plenty of it and the menus looked nice—they did Italian food region by region—

but the standard was on the poor side. Don't get me wrong, this trip was a bargain at £999 for two weeks all-inclusive with few drink restrictions and a nice outside cabin!

Celebrity Cruises Consolation
This was to places like Le Havre, Bilbao and Porto, with another few too! I got this cruise as a travel agent bargain. I invited my mum; I agreed to pay for the cruise and she paid for the all-inclusive packages, which were dear and around the same cost as the cruise.

This was a lovely ship. Due to there being a bad infection of norovirus on the previous cruise, there was a delay on embarkation in Southampton, then, once on board, a further delay in getting access to our cabin.

My premium drinks package was amazing, especially some of the Martini Bar deals. This trip was around (just after) Mum's birthday, so I treated her to one of the fine-dining restaurants one night. We had nice company at our regular restaurant table—a nice couple and also two friends who shared a cabin to keep costs down. We socialised with them a bit.

Mum liked to sit near the front of the stage for the evening shows to get a good view. One night there was this Welsh singer/comedian and, before I knew it, she'd picked me from the audience to come on stage and do this sort of singing game thing. She seemed really impressed with my voice, although my current workmates may disagree, as per my karaoke exploits!

On this cruise, we liked to go to the cinema, and there was an excellent coffee shop on board, so we would take a take-away latte in with us.

Again, really nice food on Celebrity; all in all, a really great cruise experience. Was nice to go on holiday with my mum.

P&O Cruises Ventura
Another travel agent deal. This was known as my graduation cruise as a reward for reaching the highest learning accreditation through online travel training, resulting in a significantly discounted trip.

Was interesting to get the chance to experience P&O, as this was a big seller and popular with the UK market. While most of P&O trips were from Southampton, Ventura was doing a summer sailing season off Venice.

The trip got off to a bad start. Because I was on the travel agency trip, I was not allowed to use the Glasgow to Venice charter flight and I couldn't book onto the same flight privately. KLM was the only one that connected. Problem was that when I checked in at Edinburgh airport, it printed off my two boarding passes. Edinburgh to Amsterdam was ok, but I wasn't impressed as I got a crappy middle seat because my confirmed seat booking was voided. Even worse, my Amsterdam to Venice flight never had a seat and just said "waitlist". The next flight was tight, but I would have made the latest embarkation time. I was really unimpressed with KLM overbooking and also the lack of flexibility. They refused to even look at repatriating me onto the Air France flights that had similar times and would get me there. They just said to try to resolve it in Amsterdam. I was furious. I wanted to try to relax, but I was so stressed. This was not the start you'd expect, especially having booked this flight about six months before!

I queued in Amsterdam for about thirty minutes,

then was told to queue at a second queue for another twenty minutes. The woman did un-bump me, so to speak, but seemed to think I should be hugely grateful to her for doing this! I was pleased, but the expectation is that you should be able to travel on the flight you book without all this hassle! Post-trip, KLM were a nightmare to deal with and refused to compensate me, apart from fifty pounds of miles on my loyalty card. I told them the miles were a waste of time as I wouldn't travel with them again, but they refused to send me this as cash. They stuck to these lines and told me the loyalty points were the only offer and to contact the Civil Aviation Authority if I was unhappy—not, in my view, how to deal with a complaint. I never got a single seat I had chosen, it was middle seats all the way. Probably the worst flight situation I've had!

Anyway, I got to Venice a bit stressed and had not booked any transfer to the cruise but had researched. The airport-to-city bus was cheap and straightforward and there was a funicular-type thing that then takes you near the ship. Because I was own-arrangements, I seemed to have been one of the last people to board the ship, even though it wasn't due to sail for another four or five hours. Embarkation took three minutes! No queue!

I was more than happy with my inside cabin, also saw a wee stall mentioning a free bottle of wine for early dinners at the White House (Marco Pierre White's on-board restaurant) or Sindhu (Atul Kochhar's Indian restaurant). I went to the White House, which was an amazing meal. Surprisingly, the ship left about two hours early! I reckon it would have waited for me if I had not got on the Amsterdam-Venice flight?! The views of the canals leaving Venice were amazing. The food here was incredible and the service too!

Breakfasts on board P&O cruises are a high standard. This was a similar size ship to Celebrity *Consolation*, not quite as nice as the Celebrity one, but again I liked the cinema and the Glass House wine bar. Food was good, same in the main restaurant.

Didn't really like my table here. This trip was just before the independence referendum, and there was another Scot at my table who disliked me for being pro-independence. Don't get me wrong, I've seen pro-independence people dislike others for being pro-unionist; I just feel we should, within reason, respect other people's differing opinions/ beliefs.

One of the highlights of the trip was an experience I bought, which was having dinner with the Indian Michelin-starred chef Atul Kochhar. It was a great and inexpensive experience. Unlike many of the celebrity chefs, he was calm, humble and down to earth. Had a great chat about our mutual enjoyment of food and travel!

Destination-wise, this was the Eastern Med and took me to loads of new places. A favourite was Kotor, Montenegro. Also, Corsica was great. Good to visit Dubrovnik, Croatia, for the first time since I was a child—this was part of Yugoslavia when I was there.

Overall, I enjoyed this cruise but wasn't really with like-minded people.

First trip on Fred Olsen's Black Watch
I chose this cruise because it was very well priced. For a fortnight and single cabin, this came in around a thousand pounds. This was also an all-inclusive

cruise. The destinations were nice; I had been to many of them before, such as Porto, Lisbon, Gibraltar and Hamburg amongst others.

I enjoyed the games such as table tennis and shuffleboard. Food was good, and there were some nice people. Edwina Currie was a guest speaker, talking about *Strictly Come Dancing* and politics. Despite her politics, she spoke well and was entertaining. I had a few drinks with her husband the first night at one of the bars without realising who he was. He was in an entertaining episode of *Celebrity Wife Swap*, which I watched when I got back home!

First cruise on Cruise and Maritime's Magellan. Trip to Norway.
Talked Mum and her partner, Jim, into this cruise to Norway, and they have since gone back on the same ship on two amazing long cruises. This was a cruise from Dundee – Geiranger – Flåm – Bergen – Newcastle – Dundee.

It was nice to go on holiday with Mum and Jim. We were all on all-inclusive, so could relax and enjoy a drink on the ship. I had been to Norway before, but it was good to be back.

Boarding in Dundee felt quite disorganised, but somehow, our friendly faces got us fast-tracked on board, which was a good start!

Was nice to sail from Dundee, which was another place I'd spent a few childhood years. Dinner the first two nights was interesting. There were two couples together and the three of us at the table. Some of the others didn't comply with dress code on the ship. They were all drinking like the ship was running out of wine! Also, one of the group was smoking an e-cigarette under the table.

They also hardly spoke, and it was all a bit awkward. The helpful maître d' sorted a table for three at a different restaurant for the last five nights of the cruise, and we all felt more relaxed.

Went on a nice walk in Geiranger. The setting was truly stunning, picture-postcard mountain scenery all over. We actually walked to a violin museum, which was unusual but interesting, then an art gallery.

Flåm, famous for the mountain railway and nice little railway museum, was great. I had booked the railway excursion before the trip, which made it about half price. This was truly stunning and great fun. Norway is such a picturesque country!

This was my second trip to Bergen and, as such, I made my own arrangements here. I took a funicular to a different mountain, whereas last time I had taken a cable car to another one. I walked back to the town centre, then had a smoked salmon sandwich at the fish market and an expensive beer along with it!

We just wandered about Newcastle for a few hours. The bus arrangements never really matched what we were told, but we managed to get into the city and back with only a few minor issues! I was born in Newcastle, so it was good to be back there. Usually I just change trains there! We just went for a wander and a coffee for a few hours.

Second cruise on Black Watch. Short cruise to Amsterdam and Hamburg and Bruges.
I think this was about five nights in the autumn. This was a "buy-one-get-one-free" cruise and I just took two short cruises. Enjoyed it anyway, and it was all-inclusive again with a nice outside cabin. Had a nice table, and I always enjoy going back

to Amsterdam. The overnight stays in Amsterdam and Hamburg were a bonus.

In Hamburg, I enjoyed the Wunderland miniature railway. This is actually the largest miniature railway in the world, like a huge version of Rail Riders in York, and takes about two hours to go round! This was a great and very busy attraction. I then had a wonderful lunch at a stunning parliament building. The business lunch didn't have a choice, but I was more than happy with the food, and it was about a quarter of the price of the à la carte items. It seemed like a lot of the diners were German politicians.

There were nice people on my table. Later in the cruise, we started to socialise more. The food on Fred Olsen was of a good standard.

Loved Bruges, another stunning medieval city— again, obvious comparison with York. Spent time wandering around the city and went on a brewery tour, but I didn't have time to do everything I wanted and would love to go back there again.

I had a stunning afternoon tea, while being entertained by a pianist. There was a free afternoon tea, but for the last sea day there was an option to upgrade to a premium one. I had rose-petal tea with the usual top-quality sandwiches, scones and cakes!

Also, the Future Cruise Sales agent on board was Rodger, who has actually written a cruise-related book. I'd previously met him at the Southampton Cruise Convention and enjoyed his company, so it was good to catch up with him.

Interesting thing about this cruise was that there was not another one after ours. Once we were dropped off, the ship was heading off to dry dock in Germany for refurbishment and upgrades.

Third cruise on Black Watch, a three-night cruise to Rouen.

This was one of the first cruises since the refurbishment and the ship was looking nice. Really enjoyed the scenic cruise along the River Seine. Because we were on a smaller ship, we were able to go quite far along the river into Rouen. Only a few cruise ships can do this. Again, another relaxing trip. Not as good as the previous one, but partly due to only lasting for a few nights.

Second cruise on Magellan. This was a nice itinerary involving Amsterdam, Hamburg, Copenhagen and Aalborg (Denmark).

I really liked this cruise. There were some nice folk on my table—got on really well with Dawn and Paul, I think his name was? The itinerary was great. The ship was nice and it was good to be back on my second Magellan cruise.

This time in Hamburg I did something different and went to a concentration camp. It was an emotional but interesting experience. Our guide was so humble and sombre, but very good. Was in Hamburg overnight and the next day I made the effort to go to two great beer places for my steins! Went to a lovely pub, then a huge brewery, loved them both and had two huge one-litre wheat beers!

I was also overnight in Copenhagen. Day one, I just did my own thing and wandered around the lovely city. But on day two, I met my friend William, who was one of my best friends in high school and had been living in Copenhagen for a number of years. We enjoyed loads of expensive beers in lovely settings!

In Aalborg, I managed to navigate the local bus network and went to the zoo.

I saved about half price and bought a beer passport, which gives you about five half-pint beers in different bars. This was great value, especially for Denmark, but the ship tour would have been much more expensive, and the only difference was having a guide. I enjoyed just wandering around by myself and went into four different pubs—all had nice beers, a lot of German wheat style.

Another good trip. I hoped to stay in touch with Dawn; we took each other's details but both of us seemed to be too busy.

P&O Cruises Azura. Fly cruise to the Caribbean. Barbados – St Kitts – St Lucia – Antigua – Barbados – x Azores (Medical emergency) — Southampton
Another travel agent industry deal made this exceptionally good value. I decided that the supplement for a balcony cabin was well worth paying extra for and this worked out really well.

I had a good stay at the Hilton London Gatwick. Being a Hilton Honours loyalty cardholder really makes a difference. The check-in experience was really good. Had a nice stay but ate out at a great bar at the airport that made its own gin, which was lovely!

I had been a bit worried about the long-haul flight to Barbados as it had been a good number of years since I'd travelled that sort of distance. It was a fairly good flight on Thomas Cook Airlines charter—was about an hour late, which was ok. No free alcohol, so I decided just to stick with complimentary soft drinks/coffee. Watched a few films and, after not too long, we were there. Was a good feeling to know that we would be sailing back to Southampton. I used to like long-haul flights but don't as much these days.

On landing in Barbados, there was a very early Boeing 747, coloured white with no branding, next to our flight, which looked like it was from the 1970s or possibly early '80s. This was a replacement for the 787 Dreamliner! Despite having poor facilities in terms of entertainment etc., I would have loved going on it. Apparently, there were orange and brown seats! It was also strange having buses pick us up straight off the aircraft and take us to the ship. Our luggage was being transported to our cabins.

Embarkation on the ship was busy, as lots of the flights had landed at similar times. Checked out my balcony cabin and really liked it. First thing I did, as with all ships that I hadn't been on before, was explore. Really liked it! I found the fine-dining booking table and sorted a free bottle of wine with early dining. Really enjoyed this restaurant—plenty of lobster dishes.

As we were overnight in Barbados, I went for an early bed as I had not even attempted to sleep on the flight. Managed a decent sleep and fairly early start the next morning for a hearty full-English breakfast, which was excellent on P&O. I also avoided the buffet, going for made-to-order every time!

I then headed out to see about doing some rum-tasting. With the heat, I decided to catch a taxi and sensibly agreed a fair price before going to the Mount Gay rum visitor centre. This was in a lovely historic building and there was a guided tour and generous tastings. I was not a big rum fan before the trip, but I did enjoy the tasting and now like good quality rum. Although not my favourite drink, it's a big part of the Caribbean!

After this, I went to the boatyard (a beach club with pub, restaurant and other beach facilities) but, being a weekend, it was busy. I told the receptionist I was staying in a hotel, as the free resort credit seemed better than the cruise passenger deal—although if you went for the cruise passenger deal, you got a free taxi back to the boat, saving a twenty-minute walk in the heat.

I enjoyed about four or five of the local beers. There was a free boat trip to snorkel in the sea, which I did and quite enjoyed. Sometimes, you'd see turtles, and you always see a shipwreck. The food was ok; I had the mixed battered seafood with Cajun chips. Free Wi-Fi as well.

I struggled with the walk back to the ship. I freshened up, then made my way to dinner. You paid extra to guarantee dining times and, in general, from my experience, if you preferred later times they gave you times you didn't want. I wasn't on the best of tables. There was quite a nice lady but, two nights in, she was moved to another table. One of the couples was quite nice—interesting Burmese fellow and his English wife.

St Kitts was nice; we were docked near the airport, and we did a mini-tour of the island, then headed for the Rum Train, which was quite a cool experience. Was an old Sugar Cane railway line covering much of the island. Each carriage was hosted by a barmaid, and there were singers and an island commentary. It was very expensive but a great experience and good fun. We were made amazing piña coladas and ok rum punch. This was all I did on this island.

St Lucia was my favourite island I went to, truly exotic. Here, I did a rainforest walk, which was hard going in the high-twenties heat but good fun. Didn't really see much wildlife, although I did seriously see a tarantula, which was quite a rare sight as apparently most of them get eaten by rats or snakes!

I bought some really nice rum here (coconut and banana) but had to forfeit them until the last night. The pre-cruise paperwork mentioned that you could have some drink in your cabin, but they were a bit inconsistent with the policy. I don't think they were letting any drink past them!

Lunch was included on this tour, and it was well priced but a bit plain—understandably for the price, but it would have been nice to experience more spicy Caribbean dishes. Decided for dinner to go to Sindhu, which I had really enjoyed on the previous P&O ship—a twin ship to *Azura*. Had a lovely lobster bhuna and all the usual stuff. It was so high quality; I've yet to eat in a better land-based Indian restaurant. Also wangled another free bottle of wine!

Antigua was next. My cousin Graeme had got married here, and my mum really liked this island. I didn't pre-book anything here, with the intention to walk to a beach or see what was what. I really liked the shops by the cruise terminal. It was a very well-presented centre, with lovely buildings. The taxi drivers, despite the number of ships being in, were struggling to get folk to choose their taxi. One of them pitched to me; I liked what I heard and waited for a shared taxi, which ended up really cheap, and the group of us headed for the Jolly Beach resort. It was free to go here, but I hired a deckchair. Most of the cruise passengers went via their shore excursions team. Despite the factor-fifty sun cream, I did get burned here. I enjoyed a fresh coconut with some local rum mixed in it, which was nice and cool and refreshing! Managed to sneak a bottle of kiwi cream rum liqueur back to my cabin.

After a few hours on the sun lounger, I had a disappointing meal of coconut prawns and a couple of beers. It was dear, especially considering this was only a three-star resort.

Next stop was back to Barbados and, having been frazzled in Antigua, I decided it was best to book a tour here and avoid the beach! Typically, the weather during my Caribbean cruise was high twenties to low thirties! I went on the rum distillery tour, thinking I would go to different ones. The first one was a stunning estate with an interesting history, but the tasting was stingy. I did buy a nice half-bottle of spiced rum here and managed to sneak it into my cabin. Drink prices on the ship were fair, especially when compared to the American ships, which were really expensive.

Next up was seven straight days at sea. Daytime entertainment was ok; there was a good speaker about historic and interesting murders. He was an ex-detective and actually collected things to do with historic murders. He speaks/writes so well that he's actually been on TV! There were also creative writing classes. I went to most of these but didn't enjoy them so much. Didn't rate the teacher, although she'd had some successful books published.

I quite enjoyed the table tennis; it was always doubles due to the amount of people turning up. My coordination was not great for alternative shots, and typically I would be in a team that was beaten early on and folk didn't want me as their partner. I'm much better at singles! Shuffleboard was a bit better—got to the final the last time I played this. Again, the entertainment team paired us up.

Overall, another good cruise, exceptional value, and it was nice to watch us arrive/depart while sitting in the balcony. I read about four books this cruise, which is a lot for me! I also took about seven or eight DVDs with me and got through most of these.

Travel Agent Cruise Lunches
I did a few of these while I was an active travel agent. I think my first was Holland America's (HAL) *Volendam* when it was in Greenock. It was a nice ship and our guide was very enthusiastic, advising its popularity due to being one of the smaller HAL ships. These are quieter cruise experiences, suited more to older customers. HAL is like an American version of Cunard, although they have quite a big fleet. Had a nice lunch!

Royal Caribbean's *Vision of the Seas*. Lunch in Greenock. This was the second-smallest class of RCI ship—Radiance class is the smallest. It still had a climbing wall as per all the RCI ships, and a few specialty restaurants. Another nice lunch. This was the right size of ship for me—I tend to prefer the smaller ones, as long as there are half-decent facilities.

Fred Olsen's *Boudicca*. In Rosyth, which was really handy as my sister was my chauffeur because this was only a few miles away from her Dunfermline house! It was the sister ship to *Black Watch*, which I've sailed on three times. They were both built around 1972/73. Almost identical to *Black Watch*, although *Black Watch* is the only Fred Olsen ship to currently have a cinema. It was interesting to see all the different categories of cabin. Had a lovely buffet lunch in the Garden Café.

Cruise Lines International Association (CLIA) conference, Southampton.
It was great to be at this event. I was actually

personally recognised as being one out of around twenty achieving the highest level of industry training accreditation. I had also just had my last self-employed cruise business closed due to lack of activity. This was a three-night/two-day event with useful insight into the industry and two ship visits:

Cunard's iconic *Queen Mary 2*—Was great to be on this fine ship. When built, it was the biggest in the world. Since then, there have been many bigger. Really liked it, and my mum has crossed the Atlantic on her.

Princess Cruises' *Crown Princess*—Really liked this American ship. Was able to just wander around and explore the public areas before having a lovely lunch on board. This is quite a large ship, at about 110,000 tonnes.

* * *

There is a cruise for everyone. There are affordable options, quieter options, adult-only, good family choices, boutique ships, pensioner-only ships, huge resort ships with thirty restaurants and many more.

I don't have my next cruise planned. In terms of destinations I've yet to explore by cruise, I would like to go to Alaska sometime soon-ish!

CHAPTER 11

All My Cars

I am aiming to put pictures up on the book's Facebook page of some of the cars I've owned over the years.

I continued the family tradition and passed my driving test first time, when I was just seventeen years old! I had more lessons than most of my peers, but my instructor was keen not to put me for the test until he was sure I was ready. The hardest aspects of learning to drive, to me, were clutch control and observing other drivers signalling. Thankfully, after passing my test, I have not had any serious incidents on the roads. I have had two speeding fines but, at the time of writing, have a clean licence!

Mum very kindly gave me her Y-reg (1982) Suzuki Alto (Daisy) after passing my test, which was a cute wee yellow car. I regret selling this as it was a very reliable car and a bit different.

My friend Scott was selling his blue Mini 1000 V-reg (1980) and I'd always wanted either a Mini or VW Beetle, so I sold the Suzuki and bought this. It was a bad starter in the winter and not the most reliable of cars. I ended up selling it and getting a really bad car from another friend, Colin!

Bought Colin's Ford Escort, which wasn't meant to be two-tone silver and black, 1600 X-reg (1981) for the princely sum of fifty pounds! This was even more unreliable but quite powerful—what do you expect for fifty pounds! I sold this for £180 and never spent much on it. It was a total wreck!

Bought another Mini, this time a sporty black Clubman T-reg (1979). Again, it wasn't the most reliable of cars and had a freaky tyre blow out on it!

Next up was my final Mini, and the most reliable one, a silver W-reg (1981). Sold this to my friend's partner's grandfather, and I was told the car lasted quite a few years after I sold it.

Next up was the Chevy! My blue Vauxhall Chevette X-reg (1981)—the body work was really bad, filler everywhere, but the mechanics were pretty good. I was working at a garage at the time and the mechanics were helpful and could have MOTed it for a very fair £350, with loads of welding, etc., but I decided to scrap the car—the only one I've ever scrapped.

My next one was not at all old but was truly awful—a 1989 (F-reg) Skoda Estella. It was meant to be red but the faded paint looked more orange.

Only about half the gears worked and the radiator used to overheat all the time. Managed to sell this wreck to a trader for the same price I bought it for!

My next car was a customer's trade-in that looked quite clean, a red Talbot Samba Y-reg (1982). Was a terrible starter though, and I didn't have this one long.

My next car was a cream Ford Orion 1.6 E-reg (1987). I actually got the engine changed due to a terminal oil leak. I would say this was my last bad car!

I then had a number of company vehicles. I worked for an ex-Rover garage but the car I mainly had then was a lovely, sporty, wee red Corsa SRI M-reg (1995). The garage was also an LDV van/truck dealer. As such, I sometimes took a van or even a tipper truck home!

* * *

Having lost my job at the garage, I was feeling raw and sore and thought I would try my hand at motor trading. I headed to Ingliston auctions with my car sales friend, Gary, and ended up paying about sixty pounds including buyers' fees for a rough MK1 Fiesta X-reg (1981) that seemed to drive ok but was rusty. It had an ok-length MOT and road tax. I kept this for three days before selling it for about £200! I decided not to dabble further in trade cars, despite my relative success!

My next car was a blue Austin Maestro 1.6 D-reg (1986). This was in decent nick and drove well. I used this for a Hawick-Edinburgh commute, so it had to be reliable. This one actually got written off in quite bizarre circumstances. I was doing a car boot sale in Hawick, and there was an old lady in another Maestro, a gold-coloured automatic. I was just minding my own business, busy on my stall, when I saw her driving out of control. Before I knew it, me and the other stall-holders had to move out the way as she was about to crash into my car/ the stall! My car was written off, but her insurer gave me a good price—about double what it was worth—so it all worked out ok!

I was now earning a much better salary and, with a permanent and stable job, I looked to buy my first car on finance and bought a red 2.0 Diesel Maestro J-reg (1991). It was also my first diesel car. I chose this car for improved MPG, but typical British Leyland, it wasn't built all that well. In fact, the previous Maestro was probably a better car!

Next up, I bought an early Ford Mondeo 1.8 petrol K-reg (1993), in an unusual shade of blue, from my friend Gary at Harrisons of Peebles. This was one of the best cars I've had, and I think the first one I had for over a year. Think I had this one about three years. I was doing about 25,000 miles a year, so needed something really reliable.

Next up, I stuck to Ford and went for the V6 2.5 petrol Ford Probe M-reg (1994). Not the most practical car for my high mileage, but good fun—I loved the pop-up lights! Didn't buy this from my friend's garage, and it was unreliable. Was good fun to drive though!

Next up was the first of my three Jaguars, a blue H-reg (1990) 4.0 V6 auto. Was a bit rough and only kept this a few months. This was a second car!

I was a bit more sensible with the next one. A green 1.6 petrol Ford Focus, W-reg (1999?). I bought this on eBay and picked it up south of Manchester. Kept it a few years too. I liked my ex, Karen's, Focus, which was why I got one of my own.

Alongside this, I got another second car, another Jaguar XJ6 3.2 in cream J-reg (1992). This one was an ex-wedding car. It was a nice car, if a bit rough round the edges. Head gasket was a bit iffy, but I managed to sell it ok!

I then got something a bit different again as a second car. A British racing green K-reg (1971) Rover P6 2.0. There was an article in a classic car magazine about Rover P6s that featured this one as a "usable classic". It was not dear at around £1750. I went down just south of London to collect it and made it home, although it was overrunning a bit. I only had this car for about nine months before I sold it to a real enthusiast who resprayed it pillar-box red and tidied it up. It's probably still going!

My next car was a bit more sensible. I moved on to just having the one car and bought a Ford Mondeo 1.8 LX M-reg (1994) in silver. I had this car two or three years. I sold it to a lovely young lady from Hull via eBay and delivered it to her on the condition she would pay the eighty pounds to cover fuel and a train ticket back to Scotland. Was an unusual first car for an eighteen-year-old, but she seemed happy enough.

The reason I sold it was because I wanted to get back into another luxury car and couldn't resist a British racing green Jaguar XJ6 3.2. This was in mint condition until I had a valater round and he managed to take off a bit of lacquer, which I never got sorted. It was only a minor blemish that I never even tried to claim. I kept this for around two years, and it looked stunning with my private number plate, C3DFC (yes, Dumbarton Football Club). What was great was MOTing it. I was slightly nervous, but it passed first time with no advisories! I sold this one to a guy in Germany who said he couldn't get Jaguars easily in Germany; it was all BMWs/Mercedes over there.

Briefly, alongside this, I bought a red Nissan Micra M-reg (1994) to teach people to drive in as I had started a driving instructor course. I went to the car auctions with my old college friend Bradley, and we both thought this was a tidy wee car. It was a garage trade-in, and I paid what I thought was a good price. It needed serious mechanical work as it kept cutting out, and I spent too much money on it. Got it running ok and taught a few folk at my work to drive: my friend Yvonne, and two of the graduates, Rebecca and Kate. I had got it reliable enough at this time. I MOTed it before selling, and to my horror, it needed a fair bit of welding. It was a low-mileage car, and I made sure it was in good condition when I sold it.

Having gone on to self-employment, when I saw that my friend Gary had something different in, I couldn't resist. It was a fairly high-mileage silver Saab 9-3 SE 2.0 Turbo petrol. This was a retail deal. It was late registered and was a W-reg (2000). Was in good condition, and I kept this one for about three years. Towards the end of my ownership, the brake pipes became so corroded that I had almost complete brake failure. Using the gears to slow down, I managed to avoid crashing, then the handbrake managed to stop it.

Because I was living in Glasgow, although where I was never had brilliant train/bus services, I managed without a car for about two years. There was no point having one as parking by my work was expensive, and traffic meant the train was cheaper and quicker anyway!

I kept my next car for a few years. It was a Skoda Octavia 1.8 turbo diesel 2003 (53 reg). This had about 266,000 on the clock when I bought it, as it was an ex-taxi. It was also only about five years old and cost around £775 because of the mileage. Took the decision to keep it and not scrap it about the third year I had it. MOT was bad at a cheaper garage—had a cutting-out issue and the driveshaft had gone. Should have scrapped it, as the bill came in at around £1000. Typically, I'm ok paying £500 for an MOT with all the repairs! The final straw was it getting badly vandalised in the Eastgate car park, Peebles. My flatmate's expensive, pride-and-joy motorbike was also vandalised. I had a massive dent on the side and smashed passenger side window. One other vehicle was damaged as well. Police were disinterested.

I took this car over 300,000 miles on its last journey to Birmingham. It was literally dying on the way down. Occasionally, there'd be a big random misfire and huge cloud of black smoke! MPG went from fifty-five to twenty-five on this trip, but I just gritted my teeth and somehow made it!

After that, I couldn't resist another luxury car. I bought a dark blue Chrysler 300 CRD 3.0 Turbo diesel 08 (2008). Again, it was a fair trek to Birmingham to collect it. Unless I buy from a more well-known/reputable garage, I probably won't do this again. I had asked the right questions (e.g. any blemishes/issues—no!) and it was a good price, but when I collected it, there were 30,000 more miles on the clock than advertised. There was significant lacquer damage on one of the wheel arches. I think I got an extra £300 off it—I was quite pissed off, though given my old car was a mess, I decided to take the new car. Incidentally, they gave me £500 for mine with a week's MOT.

The Chrysler drove amazingly, but the lights

failed. It was either full-beam or no lights. Got my mechanic friend to look over it and he advised me of a few things. Even the lights were expensive zeon lights. I decided to liaise with my bank/trading standards, and I got about another £500 back, which was a good result and made me the winner after the issues I'd encountered! My intention with this car was to run a chauffeur business called Mr Bentley (as the car looked like a Bentley—was that dodgy?) with it, but that never worked out. I enjoyed this car for about two years, but it was way too expensive to run. I ended up selling it privately. It had a reoccurring automatic gear issue, sometimes getting stuck in first gear. I got this fixed a few times and decided it was time to sell while this was working ok. I did the sale in a Carlisle car park to a guy from Bradford—this was roughly the halfway point. The boot was stuck shut, which I had disclosed. Never heard back from the buyer, so hopefully the gear issue didn't actually reoccur.

My next car was my first ever brand-new car. A white Dacia Sandero 1.5 Diesel 15 (2015). Getting a brand-new car was a great feeling, but picking it up was stressful, as the salesman, who was a nice fellow, forgot to tell me all the documents I needed. I brought what I thought was needed, but when he asked, "Have you brought this and that?" No and no! The sales manager resolved this—thankfully, as I was car-less, having sold the Chrysler privately. I got an amazing deal: £8,600 with extended five-year warranty (50,000 miles) and three free services. This included a £500 dealer incentive. While the same model is still good value, these are now about £10,000 new. It was a great reliable car. I only kept it two-and-a-bit years and traded it in at 46,000 miles.

My next car is my current car, a Corsa 1.3 turbo diesel in yellow. 12-reg (2012), only 31,000 on the clock. At the test drive, I noticed the engine warning light was on, but I wasn't hugely worried about this. On agreeing to buy it, I said that they had to sort the engine warning light and put it through the workshop, service and MOT. Sale included a year's warranty and two services/MOTs. It cost my car plus £1000. This might not have looked a great deal, but this was well spec'd, in my favourite colour and immaculate. Looked in better nick than the Dacia. I called just before sorting the insurance, asking if my car was ready—yes! On arriving at the garage, the salesman sheepishly told me the engine warning light was still on, and they had organised for me to take it to a rival dealership to clear, which would only take five minutes. The next day, I had a three-hour hang around the rival garage, and they still couldn't sort it. I was furious! Two courtesy cars and about three weeks later, the car was mine again. Since then, the car has been reliable—only real issue has been two punctures, and it needed a spring at MOT, which would have been about £300 but was covered by the warranty.

In the last four years or so, I've moved away from big, fuel-guzzling luxury cars to more economical ones. However, due to the 20,000 annual miles, and the fact that the last few winters have been quite bad, this autumn I'm hoping to get a Dacia Duster 4x4.

CHAPTER 12

Number One Sons (Dumbarton FC) supporter

My mum's cousin Donald McNeil signed for Dumbarton from junior football in 1975. To date, he is the longest-serving Dumbarton player and well in the top ten for appearances.

My first game was when Dad took me to a reserves game that we lost about 8-1 to Dundee United; but, as a four- or five-year-old, I liked all the goals and was not too worried about which team scored them! Donald got a nasty leg injury that game. Was told this was in the late 1970s—I would have only been young, but I remember the game!

My next game, and the first one I watched

with the first team, Dumbarton beat Dundee 2-1 in the Premier division season 1984/85—the only season in my lifetime that Dumbarton have been in the top flight! It was a great day out with the family—Mum, Dad, Carole and a family friend, Douglas. At the end of the game, I got my programme autographed by the players, and when Donald met us, he turned me into a Dumbarton supporter. He gave me a behind-the-scenes tour. It was great to see the changing rooms and meet the legendary Mr Dumbarton (groundsman and more), Dick Jackson. The manager, Davie Wilson, was very happy to have us visit him in the manager's office. This behind-the-scenes tour was a real treat to a young lad and, from then on, I was a big Dumbarton fan.

I remember, as a kid, one year at Christmas I got a full Dumbarton strip—was my best Christmas present. That was around the time the club was in the premier division.

Dad would occasionally take me and a friend to a game. Even playing lower league teams in cup ties, from the 1980s until about five or six years ago, we had a dreadful record. Dad would take me to two or three games a season.

When I was in my fourth year at high school, my parents were ok about me spending my pocket money going to games. Following his retirement as a player, my mum's cousin had stayed on at the club. He had been caretaker assistant manager, then coach. His involvement was handy, as either he or his dad would give me complimentary tickets for any home games. My friends Gary and Grant often took the crazy mix of bus, train and train through from Peebles with me—around four and a half hours round-trip! It was a good day out, but we would spend twenty or thirty pounds each, so it was a lot of money in the late '80's/early '90s for a kid.

Towards the end of the club's time at our old ground, Boghead, I would go to a lot of games. This was around the mid-1990s. I went to most games from 1997 until about 2005.

I remember going to Brockville in the mid-1990s for a Dumbarton v Falkirk, and Falkirk were in such a financial mess that there were rumours that the game may be off up until a few hours before kick-off. Falkirk got through the financial issues, mainly caused by top-flight clubs then having to be all-seater stadiums. Many clubs have since gone through similar difficulties.

Season 1994/1995 was particularly memorable as this was the Murdo Macleod player/manager era, and we got promoted on the last game of the season, finishing as runners up. We were away to Stirling Albion and it was like a cup final as the winner of the game would be promoted to what was the Scottish First division—which is the second tier in Scottish football—along with champions Morton. Dumbarton won 2-0.

Murdo started the following season really well and had a few notable wins early on, which was noticed by Partick Thistle. Sadly, his highly successful era at the helm was coming to an end.

I can remember one of the most exciting wins was 1-0 at home to Dundee United. This game was on 7 October 1995 and is on YouTube. It was all Dundee United but, somehow, we scored against the run of play and held on. There was also a game where a well-known player, Chic Charnley, actually scored from the halfway line, seeing the keeper was vulnerable.

This season was all downhill after that. My mum's neighbour and friend Stuart took me to the next away game at Dundee United, and they hammered us 8-0. Stuart certainly enjoyed that! We actually never won another game that season and finished bottom by a mile.

We didn't win another game, home or away, for the rest of this season, conceding ninety-nine goals, but at least avoiding a hundred! Our next competitive win was eleven months later. It was a really grim time, and we were too slow to change manager. Jim Fallon had taken over from Murdo, and he was a nice fellow but not the best manager. He became a highly respected physio.

The next season did not fare much better, finishing ninth and getting a double relegation. It was really grim to watch. The following season was much the same, and we actually finished bottom of the bottom division.

My loyalty was tested, but you never change your football team.

Season 1999/2000 brought a bit more hope and re-enthused me. My old schoolfriend Andy Brown had signed; he had been at full-time rivals Clydebank, who were in financial trouble and actually soon got taken over by the new Airdrie owner, who relocated the club and renamed them Airdrie United.

Dumbarton were going through an exciting chapter and were moving to a new stadium the following season. A few months before the season finished, one of my friends, Alan, who has since become a club director, invited me to join him and a few others in sponsoring the last ever match at Boghead. It was great to be involved in football history, as on the day of this game, Dumbarton had played longer at the same ground than anyone else in the UK. The match-day hospitality was amazing. I bought a bottle of commemorative whisky, which has remained unopened. My mum's cousin Donald was also at the game, as well as other past players. The player of the year awards followed. I took a little bit of turf as a memento, but this has since been lost.

The following season started nervy as the club were homeless, mainly due to delays in the new stadium being completed. We were temporarily playing our home games at Albion Rovers, Cliftonhill—a traditional old ground not dissimilar to Boghead. However, I had bought a part-hospitality season ticket, which meant that when the new stadium opened, I would have lunch and a half-time "bun-fight" at every home game. For the small premium involved, this was a great option and the games felt that bit more special.

The official opening was a game against a strong Rangers team; following that, it was Elgin City, whom we beat in the first ever competitive game there.

Towards the end of this season, there was definitely a lot of optimism.

Over the summer, such was my enthusiasm that I responded immediately when my renewal request came through. Weeks later, to my total surprise, I received in the post season ticket number one! I think I'd had number eight the previous season. Not sure if this was an act of kindness to me by the CEO, Gilbert Lawrie, whom I was friends with and who sadly died a few years ago, or whether it was just the case that I applied for my ticket mega early. Every supporter would dream of holding season ticket number one!

One of my favourite games took place this season, a 5-4 win away to Stirling Albion. One minute we were losing, the next we would be winning. It was jerseys for goalposts stuff!

I made some lifelong friends around this era. I met my friend Mark coming back from Berwick Rangers. We were both waiting on the train and got chatting and we had a few mutual friends. He is such a good friend that I was honoured to be at his wedding, and I've also been to his eldest daughter's christening. Mark introduced me to Alan, as they invited me to the club's quiz night to form a team. The other member of our team was one of the players' dads.

The following season, the club stopped doing the hospitality tickets. Myself, Mark, Alan and his dad, Harry, would meet up in Glasgow before every home game, and often afterwards too, and enjoy some beers. This was more fun, as was the like-minded company.

This was also a promotion-winning season, having been runners up. It was a really good feeling at the end of this season.

The manager, Tom Carson, who was also a former player, never saw eye-to-eye with the board of directors and left the club. This was a shame, as he was a real people person and had got the best out of the team.

The next season saw us just avoid relegation. Another change of manager to Brian Fairley during this season saw more positive times, although sadly, at the end of Brian's first season, he made some changes in personnel, and my good friend Andy moved to Stenhousemuir.

Pre-season, we had a Stirlingshire cup tie away at Falkirk, who were ground sharing with

Stenhousemuir and made the unwise decision to allow free entry. Despite arriving about twenty or thirty minutes before kick-off, the ground was at capacity and I never got in. The chap who was next to me suggested we should go for a beer and head back towards full-time. John became another lifelong friend; he was particularly disappointed not to get in, as his son, Chris, who became a fan favourite, was making his debut for the club. After a few beers, we headed back to the game just in time to watch the penalties, as it had been a draw.

The following season, we just missed out in promotion to the second tier of Scottish football. Again, our manager left for Forfar, and things went downhill again—in fact leading to relegation in 2008/2009. This was the Paul Martin era.

We had three seasons in the bottom division, but it was still an enjoyable period. Some of the smaller grounds are my favourites—Brechin City and Berwick Rangers are two of my favourite away days. Chris left the club the season we got relegated, but only as he was moving to Australia for a year or so.

One of my favourite adventures was a pre-season friendly to Billingham Town. I had helped organise a deal at a Middlesbrough hotel where most of the supporters stayed, which worked out well and was a great experience. It was also unusual for the club to travel to England for a friendly.

A few managers later, it was Jim Chapman who took the club back to the second division, but things were tough in the second division, and he was soon replaced by his assistant manager, Alan Adamson.

In Alan's first full season, he took us to fourth position, which qualified us for the then fairly new play-offs. Having narrowly won a double-header semi-final v Arbroath, I remember going to the home first leg of the final play-off, and we beat Airdrie 2-1, taking a slight lead before the big away leg. This clashed with my Baltic cruise to Russia— in fact, I was in Tallinn, Estonia, on the day of the second leg, and I avoided hearing the result. I had instructed my flatmate to record the game, and the first thing I did when I got back from my cruise was get a few beers out and watch the game. This was amazing; I loved the ALBA coverage in Scottish Gaelic. Our striker Craig Dargo had an amazing game, and the second leg was a 4-1 victory, taking the club back to the second tier of Scottish football for the first time in around fifteen years.

Bizarrely, even though Airdrie lost, they ended up getting promoted due to the demise of Rangers, who ended up being demoted to the third division.

Following a not-unexpected dreadful start to the season, Dumbarton parted company with Alan Adamson. His replacement was amazing—former Hibs and Rangers player Ian Murray. He set the heather alight with an amazing run of games and, somehow, we avoided the drop—was like a miracle!

The following season, he continued the great change in fortune, and we actually went into the last game of the season with an outside chance of promotion to the Scottish Premiership, but we narrowly lost to Dundee. We ended up winning and losing fifteen games, therefore only drew six games, which really took advantage of the three points for a win. The highlight this season was an amazing Scottish Cup run. The away trip to Aberdeen in the Scottish Cup quarter final remains one of my favourite away days, narrowly losing 1-0 late in the game.

The following season, the now-known-as Championship was extremely exciting and competitive with Rangers, Hibs and Hearts all in the division—this won't ever happen again! It was great watching Dumbarton. Hearts won the league well ahead of Rangers, who never made it through the play-offs. Dumbarton managed one draw against Hearts and two great wins against Hibs; our record against Hibs has been really good the last few years!

So, the following season was another one with big teams, and with Iain Murray now off to St Mirren, which never worked out well for him, we had another new manager—this time Stevie Aitken, who had done very well with a limited budget at Stranraer. I was really pleased with this appointment.

He had two seasons of just avoiding the drop, with Dumbarton usually being one of two part-time clubs. For a good five years, Dumbarton had the title of Scotland's best part-time team, but in 2017-18 we finally went down to the first division, now the third tier of Scottish football. This season wasn't all gloom and doom, as we enjoyed the club's first cup final in my lifetime (not counting the Stirlingshire Cup). The previous final was the St Mungo's Quaich in 1951-1952, and before that the Scottish Cup in 1896-97! We had been starved of decent cup runs in recent times.

Unfortunately, my holiday in Malta again clashed with our semi-final win at The New Saints (known as TNS), a club based in Oswestry, England, a few miles from the Wales border, that play in the Welsh league, qualifying for Europe every year. They are a bit like the Welsh league version of Celtic, although they don't have a big fan-base. In fact, there were more Dumbarton supporters than TNS ones! It was a long journey made by somewhat optimistic Dumbarton supporters.

The game was on Welsh TV. I had made efforts to watch it in Malta—I thought I could link on to my Sky anywhere, but a few days before the game, I discovered that the "anywhere" was anywhere within the UK. I persuaded the hotel bar manager to show the match; I gave him the details, and he told me that was fine. I went to the hotel bar thirty minutes before kick-off and was told they didn't have the channel. I was already prepared for this response, and Bet365 came to the rescue—they had live-streaming and all I had to do was place a bet. I got ten pounds at twelve-to-one. It streamed in about a quarter of my monitor and I couldn't enlarge it—I was just grateful to watch it at all! TNS were all over us, but Dumbarton's defence held out in the first half. There were live odds changing all the time. By the start of the second half, the Dumbarton price for a normal-time win had changed to forty-to-one, and then in the fifty-second minute, TNS took an expected lead. The odds changed to 120-to-one. I didn't want the distraction of placing a further bet, but I had a good feeling, and yes! Danny Handling, previously of Hibs, scored about twenty minutes later and, with about ten minutes of the game left, our Cyprus international, Dimitris Froxylias, known either as Jimmy or Froxy, scored a wonderful goal. You should YouTube it if you've not seen it—it really was something special. Dumbarton reached the cup final, something I never thought I would experience in my lifetime!

Inverness also had a tough game against Northern Ireland's Crusaders to reach the final. It was good to see both the Scottish teams making the final, as it would have been strange to see a non-

Scottish club winning a Scottish trophy—although I do like the guest teams; it creates great football fan adventures. Many Dumbarton supporters state the trip to Oswestry was their favourite game.

I had only got back from my Caribbean cruise the night before the final and it was a relief not to miss it. I put yellow, black and white face paint on and really soaked up the atmosphere of Perth city centre. I met my pals at the Wetherspoons as we talked about the occasion. It was a backs-to-the-walls defensive strategy, much like we'd used almost every game of the season. We had a tough cup run from the first round v Rangers U21s, with several first-team players in the squad, then full-time Raith Rovers, an extra-time win against the delightfully named Welsh runners-up, Connah's Quay Nomads! It was a last-minute goal that gave Inverness the deserved victory. It was great to be there, and hopefully we can get to the final again, perhaps going one step further and winning the cup!

I'm not sure of the impact of our cup run, but last season (2017/18), we played a record number of competitive matches—over fifty—and this, without a doubt, contributed to a poor second half of the league season. The first half of the season, we had been ahead of both Falkirk and Inverness, but being a part-time team, the campaign took its toll on the team. We finished the season well ahead of minnows Brechin, who didn't win a league game the entire season, but we were having to face the play-offs for the second time. A narrow and undeserved two-legged win over Arbroath took us to the final, and we were to play Alloa.

I decided to watch the first leg from home, and I would say Dumbarton had a 1-0 win against the run of play. Both legs of the final were on BBC Alba. I went to the second leg and it was 0-0 (1-0 to Dumbarton on aggregate) one minute from full-time, and Alloa got the deserved goal to take the game into injury time. They were all over us and, despite some great match-winning players on the bench, the manager made poor defensive changes and the extra-time outcome was inevitable. Dumbarton's five-year spell in the 2nd tier of Scottish football was over, and Alloa took our long-held crown of Scotland's best part-time football club.

Hopefully we can bounce back in the next season or two and be better to watch, playing more attractive, attacking football.

CHAPTER 13

Politics

I've had an interest in politics since even before I was an adult. I believe that supporting a political movement is nothing like following a football team. With changes to yourself, the policies of the political party, peer persuasion, moral and ethical choices, considering voting for a different party can be the right decision. Growing up in the Scottish Borders, it was always a Liberal Democratic stronghold until the mid-1990s. Lord Steel was our MP for much of my time living in Peebles.

A big influence on me was my enjoyment of modern studies at high school. This was my favourite subject. We studied Communist Russia and the Cold War extensively. I was also the Labour candidate at our third-year mock general election. I gave a speech on video that my class teacher Mrs Muirhead talked positively about.

I've previously supported the Lib Dems, although that was partly down to accessing a full-sized snooker table at the Liberal Club in Galashiels! I did enhance my support by doing a little bit of phone canvassing when I moved to Edinburgh.

When the coalition government with the Conservatives and Lib Dems occurred, I decided to consider the options. This was due to a number of policies being given up—not least free university course fees. While Scotland was separate, I felt this was too much, and I then started to think more about Scotland's future.

Despite being English-born, I started to feel more patriotic. This was in 2010 and I felt Scottish rather than British. I also liked how the SNP were running Scotland.

I joined the SNP at this time but, despite being a party member, I never found my local councillor particularly helpful in resolving noise issues with a nearby pub. I got involved at meetings and helped with leafleting for election campaigns for both Holyrood and Westminster.

I felt that my consumer champion/trade union skills, and the fact that I was always looking to help people and ensure fairness, meant I could become a councillor.

I resigned from the SNP as my opinion was that local councils worked well on an apolitical basis, so it was my ambition to be an independent councillor. I discussed this with family and friends two or three years before the election came around. I think people were surprised that I actually went ahead and stood.

I really made an effort. My friend Alan kindly helped me with the design of a leaflet. I leaflet-dropped around 4,000 leaflets, covering almost every property in the ward I was standing in. There had been a number of controversial decisions made about things like the Scottish Tapestry and 4G pitches. I also supported a return to free garden waste disposal.

I enjoyed engaging with the public and received a positive response at people's doors. The hustings, while daunting, were great fun, and I was happy to do more than get through it. At times, it felt like

I was back in a show on stage! I felt I was able to use humour and enjoyed the experience. A good number of people pledged their votes on the back of this!

I set myself a number of targets: first, to do better than the independent candidate at the last election, which was actually a by-election in 2013, when both the independent candidate and UKIP candidate received forty-three votes each on first preference. In 2017, I almost doubled that to seventy-three first preferences. However, the other independent candidate, Tommy, got about twice as many votes as me. It was nice to bump into people who told me they had voted at least first, second or third preference for me. I loved the experience and at least avoided humiliation! It was always going to be a battle between the SNP and Conservatives for the first seat. The Lib Dems scraped the third seat, entirely down to proportional representation. Had it been first past the post, there would have been two Conservatives and one SNP. There was mostly good camaraderie between the candidates. The downside was essentially that the Conservatives' leaflets throughout Scotland were all about an independent Scotland being bad, and persuading people to vote Tory to avoid this, despite the fact it was a local election and nothing to do with Scottish independence. This really made it SNP v Conservatives. Though it was good for Kris, the Lib Dem candidate, to get the third seat.

After this, I decided to return to a party, but this time, I've actually joined the Scottish Green party. I have a lot of time for the people at local and Scottish level and felt this was a like-minded movement that matched many of my own beliefs. We do need to take better care of our planet. While many of the Greens' views and policies match the SNP's, I feel this is more me at this time. Like I say, I will support/get involved with a political party that matches me, and I don't know how long I will be a member of Scottish Greens—could be for life or a few years. I wouldn't rule out supporting any other party in the future, apart from the Conservatives!

Will I stand in another Local Council Election? Who knows. At this time, I would consider standing either as a Green or independent candidate but will review this at the time of a future opportunity. Living in Galashiels, I would need to consider whether I would stand in Gala or Tweeddale West again, or East.

In general, politics has gone mad, gone volatile, and there is a lot of hate. It is hard to understand how Donald Trump has become the president of America. The situation changes all the time. There have been recent worries about a possible return to a cold war, but things have quietened again! The UK has managed to avoid the worst of the far-right with UKIP and the BNP all but vanishing, but there are the current worries about leaving the EU. Brexit is a mess. Could this trigger Scottish Indy Referendum Number Two?

CHAPTER 14

The Future

So here we are! Just, firstly, thank you so much for reading my story. I do hope it has inspired you and that you have found it interesting or relevant.

While I am no celebrity and have not achieved anything huge, I do feel that when I consider the obstacles that have been in my way, I am happy with what has happened and where I am now.

I would actually say that my greatest achievement in life has been writing this book. The process from deciding to write it to actually doing so was not easy. It has taken me just under four years to complete this, although most of the writing has taken place in the last year.

I have learnt from many mistakes I have made along the way in my forty-four years! My travel experiences have not been cheap, and my past inability to manage money has been a challenge.

I am, however, proud that I took a deep breath about three years ago and mainly worked my way out of debt. Including commuting time, a typical working week is seventy hours long!

I am now starting to change my focus from debt to wealth and am looking to build up a portfolio of buy-to-let properties. I am aiming to build this up gradually and hope to start with one and see how that goes. I am targeting a nearby town were yields are as high as ten to thirteen percent. If I'm paying about £140 a month but getting in £275, this is a decent pot, and at the point that I've repaid (approximately twenty years) this should become a great investment and will hopefully help secure a decent retirement in around twenty years (from 2018).

I would like to have a partner but through lack of time, etc., I have neglected this area.

I am working hard on weight loss. I have lost over a stone and a half in the last six months. I'm halfway there—I have gone from "obese" to "overweight", and the next step is to move my BMI from "overweight" to "normal". I have settled into a routine where for breakfast I have a Herbalife shake with semi-skimmed milk. For lunch, I have a healthy meal and avoid processed foods. For dinner, I have a Huel, which is an oaty protein shake that you just add water to. I have hit a routine with these that I never managed in previous attempts and think I will stay with this for a while. I have also had a number of personal training sessions, which have helped. Tying in with my weight loss, I would like to do another marathon. In fact, I would like to do Edinburgh and give London a third and last go. My personal training has gone quite well, but I'm nowhere near the point of being able to jog nonstop for extended periods of time.

I would like to walk the Southern Upland Way but not camp—would need to be B&Bs and hotels. Possibly I'd also like to do the West Highland Way for a second time.

I would like to continue my travels and would like to cruise Alaska. Closer to home, I would like to cruise or even drive to the Isles of Skye, Mull, Shetland, Barra and Orkney. I would also like to try a luxury cruise; I'm thinking Oceania Cruises.

I would actually like to visit North Korea; I think there is something interesting about a country stuck in time and under a now-rare communist regime. I know this is unusual, but that's just me!

I would like to perform in a Fringe Festival show. I have looked into the possibilities of ventriloquism; however, the coordination of this may prove too tricky. I was inspired by one of the performers on my last cruise and have also since gone to see Nina Conte at Borders Book Festival in Melrose. The human ventriloquist is of particular interest— it's totally hilarious! Google it!

Career-wise, I would like to continue to have a travel sideline in some way, shape or form. I am pondering another home-based retail thing that would allow me to get future familiarisation trips/ cruises without the need for me to be an amazing seller.

I am enjoying the new prospects of being a company-wide dyslexia/dyspraxia ambassador in my main job, and the input I may have helping like-minded fellow employees. I'm not sure if I will get back in a managerial role in the future, but I will continue to go for these opportunities as I truly believe that I'm a people person and can help to get the best out of people.

I may also dabble in car trading, but on a self-employed basis, doing it properly with trade plates and trader insurance, one car at a time.

I hope that you will go on to my book's Facebook page, which you should be able to easily find just by searching for Yellow Spaghetti. You don't need to be a member of Facebook to access this page.

I would like to thank my mum for designing the excellent front cover and for her input in polishing it up a bit, with my understandable poor grammar and spelling! She has worked so hard on my project.

I wish you all the very best too. Get in touch with me to tell me what you thought of the book!

AUTHOR PROFILE

Michael Needham was born in 1974 and has mainly lived in the Scottish Borders. Michael is a long-suffering Dumbarton Football Club supporter and has travelled the world several times and cruised extensively. At the time of writing, he is single, and is very proud to have written his first book!

Michael is a GMB Trade Union representative and has recently become a company-wide ambassador for dyslexic and dyspraxic employees.

He hopes you will enjoy his story and may be inspired. There have not been many books about the personal experiences of adults who have recently discovered they are dyslexic or dyspraxic.

Publisher Information

Rowanvale Books provides publishing services to independent authors, writers and poets all over the globe. We deliver a personal, honest and efficient service that allows authors to see their work published, while remaining in control of the process and retaining their creativity. By making publishing services available to authors in a cost-effective and ethical way, we at Rowanvale Books hope to ensure that the local, national and international community benefits from a steady stream of good quality literature.

For more information about us, our authors or our publications, please get in touch.

www.rowanvalebooks.com
info@rowanvalebooks.com

Lightning Source UK Ltd.
Milton Keynes UK
UKHW041348131218
333957UK00003B/388/P